KNOW THY ~~F*cking~~ Awesome SELF

An Infinite Journal of Exploration and Play

BY WYOH LEE

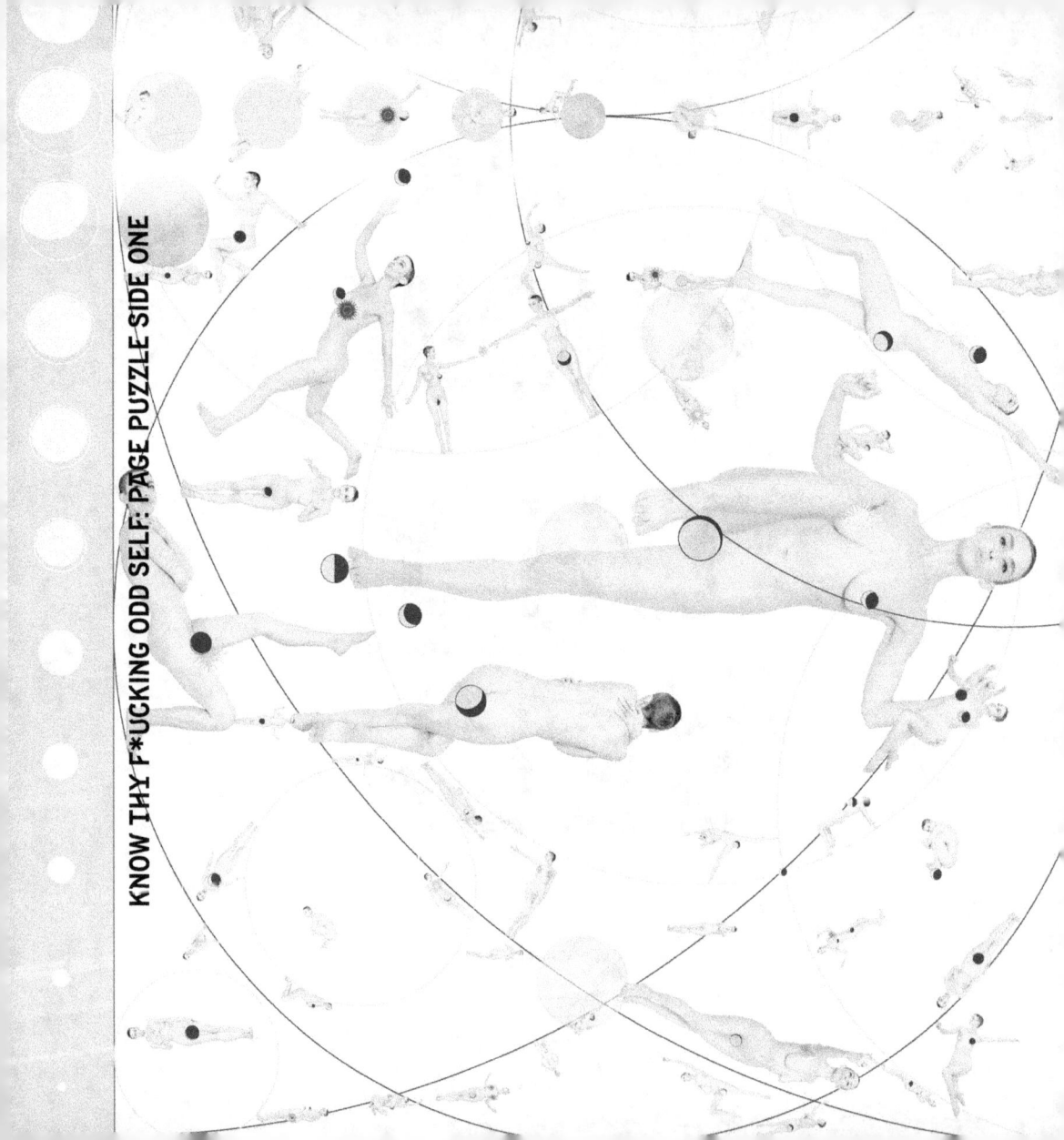

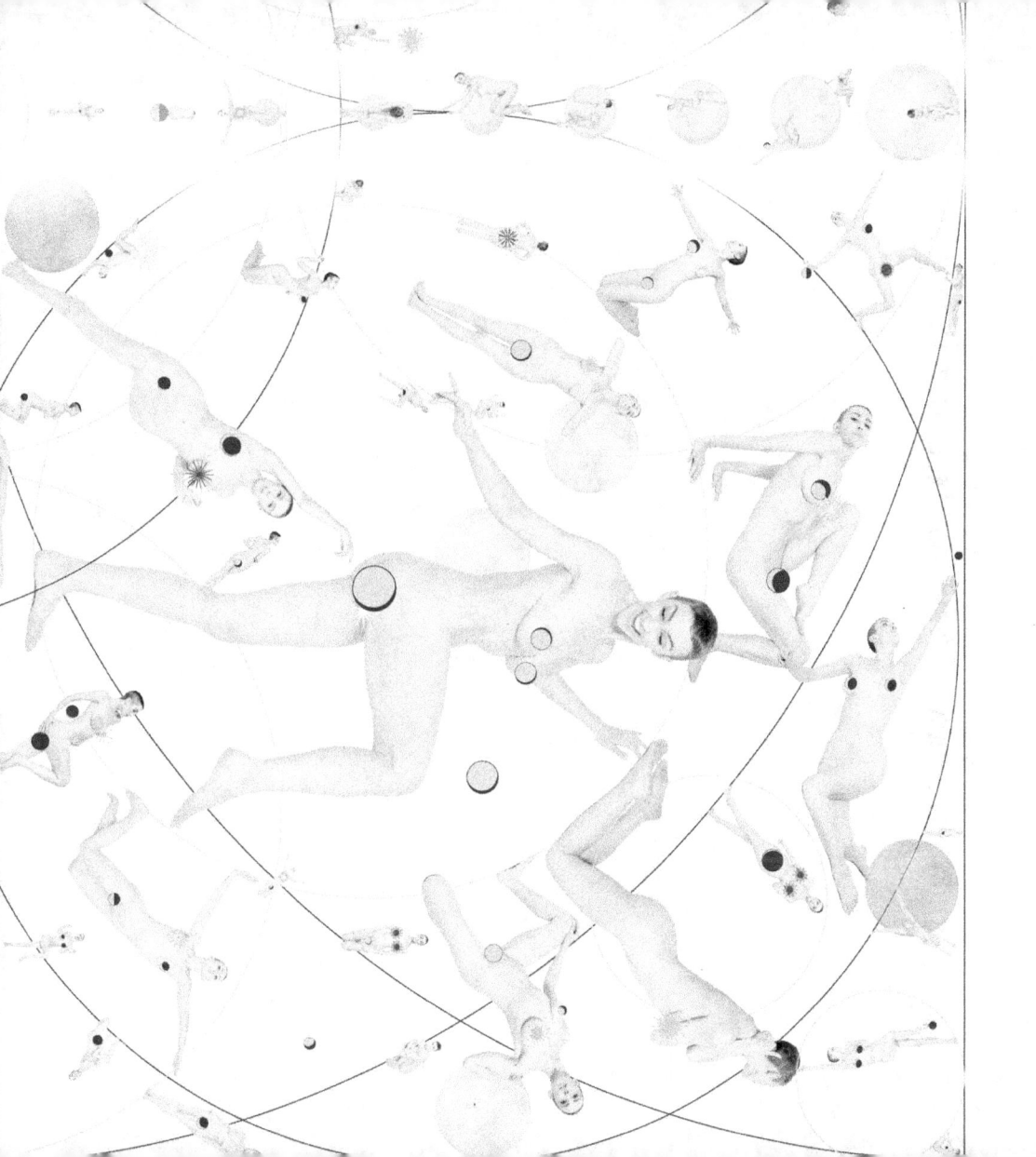

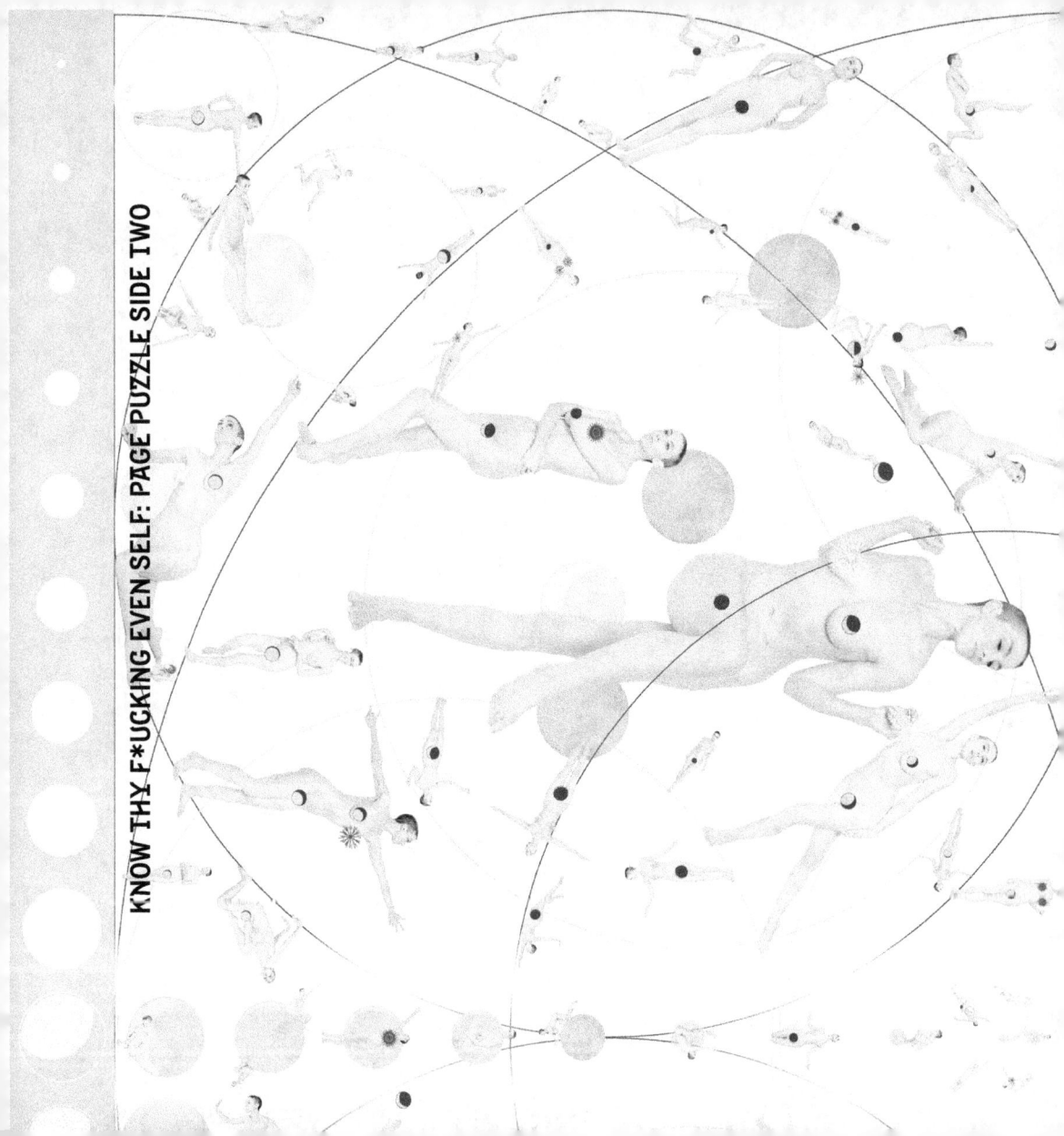

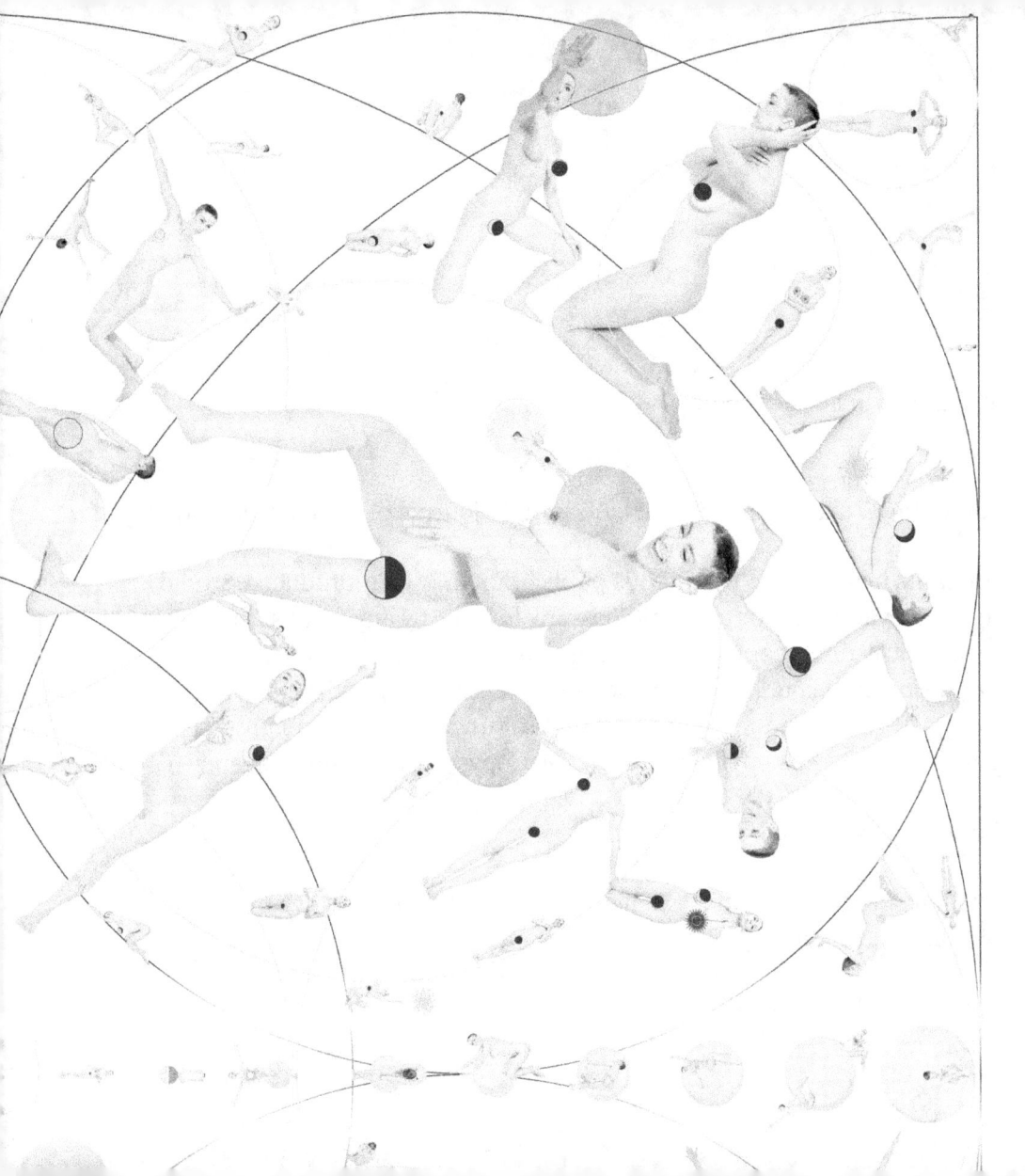

© 2021 Karin Lee Schneider

Wyoh Lee
Know Thy F*cking Awesome Self: An Infinite Journal of Exploration and Play

All rights reserved. No part of this publication may be reproduced, stored in a retrieval system or transmited in any form or by any means, electronic, mechanical, photocopying, recording or otherwise without the prior permision of the publisher or in accordance with the provisions of the Copyright, Designs and Patents Act 1988 or under the terms of any licence permitting limited copying issued by the Copyright Licensing Angency.

Published by: Wyoh Media

A CIP record for this book is acailable from the Library of Congress Cataloging-in-Publication Data

ISBN-13: 978-1-7366178-0-9

Los Angeles, CA

FOR MOM & DAD

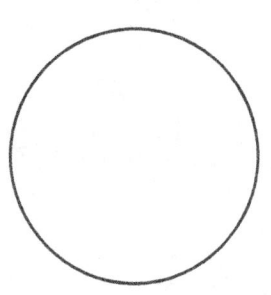

HOW TO USE THIS BOOK

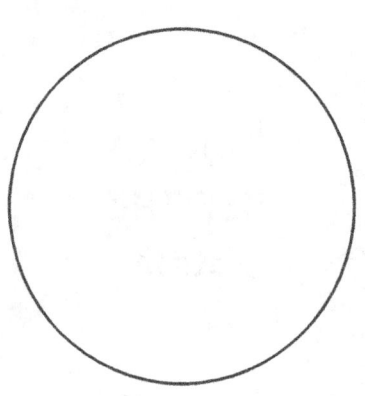

One page a day.

Notice what you love, what you hate, what you want to change. **Keep a list** of the things that ignite you. **Roll your eyes** as-needed.

Or don't.

Set a timer for one minute and **let the question simmer** in your mind.

Set a timer for fifteen minutes and **write without stopping**.

Set a timer for as long as you have and spend it however sparks **pleasure**.

Write in this book.
Jot down thoughts.
Write a story, write a poem, write
the thing you wish were true.

Draw the hope.
Doodle the feeling.
Paint a picture.
Pick and choose.

Rip out the pages.
Make paper airplanes.

Crumple them up and play
wastebasketball. Un-crumple them and
make a giant puzzle.

Scratch out the stupid parts.
Scribble on the pages.
Share and rewrite as-needed.

Let your pen
or pencil
or crayon
or marker
or fingers
or voice
or body
do the thinking.

Let your ideas be WILD.
Let your logic brain rest
(unless it brings you pleasure).

How many details you can give?
Get curious.

YOU ARE
FUCKING
AWESOME.

Give yourself permission

   to take only what excites you.
  to be human
 for pleasure
to grow
to let yourself feel
how
 fucking
  awesome
   you really are.

You, yes, you.

If letting
yourself shine is the
greatest gift you can
give humanity, what
personal revolution is
it time to spark
now?

There is a spark of revolution inside of you. What is it?

How has celebrating yourself this year brought you closer to others?

Know Thy F*cking Awesome Self | 2

We all have weird parts. When do you like letting yours out?

What
nourishment
would you
like to
offer the
world?

Know Thy F*cking Awesome Self | 4

A grand party is thrown in your honor and it's perfect. What's it like?

When you realize
you're stuck
in your head,
how do you
make
your
way
back
to
heart
connection?

Know Thy F*cking Awesome Self | 6

It's an evening of enjoyment with a handful of people you love. Details, please?

Tell
the
story
of
group
mischief
you
gleefully
joined.

When does silence comfort you?

When is it effortful?

If you could send a message to the whole wide world, what would you say?

The
time
has
come
to write
you-know-who
a
goodbye
letter.

What will you say?

Describe the beauty of your eccentricity.

Tell the story of a wordless communication makes your heart flutter.

Tell a story of melting into those around you, and feeling bliss.

You live in the household of your dreams. What does it look like?

When you are aloof and stubborn, what's the antidote?

Where's a place in the world that feels like home, though you do not live there?

How will you share your great love with humanity?

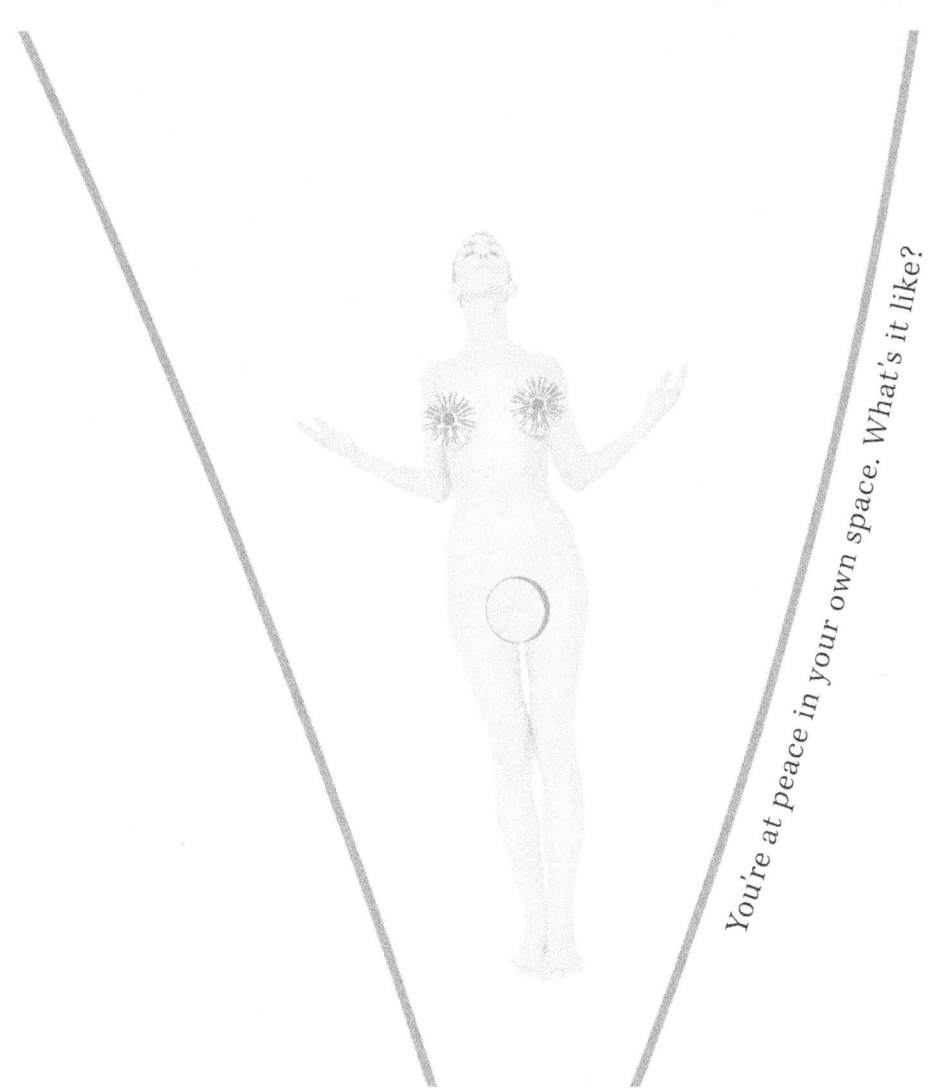

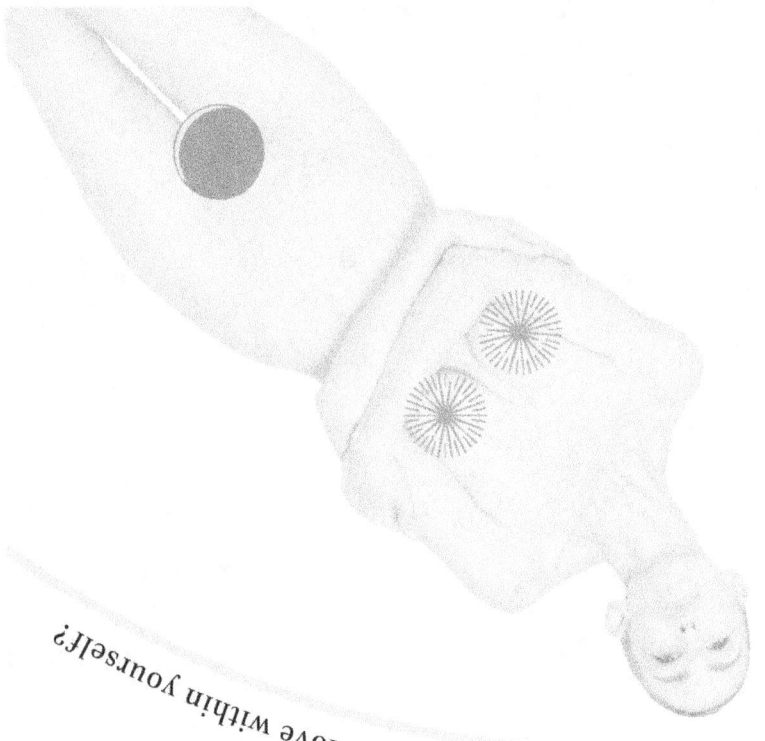

How do you grow the biggest love within yourself?

Could you, would you make silent, playful eyes at strangers? Have you?

Brainstorm a new way to welcome endings.

Your hidden creative self comes out to play. What do you do together?

When have you cried with strangers?

How does your to-do list make you feel?

What is it time to edit, complete, delete?

How do you rebel?

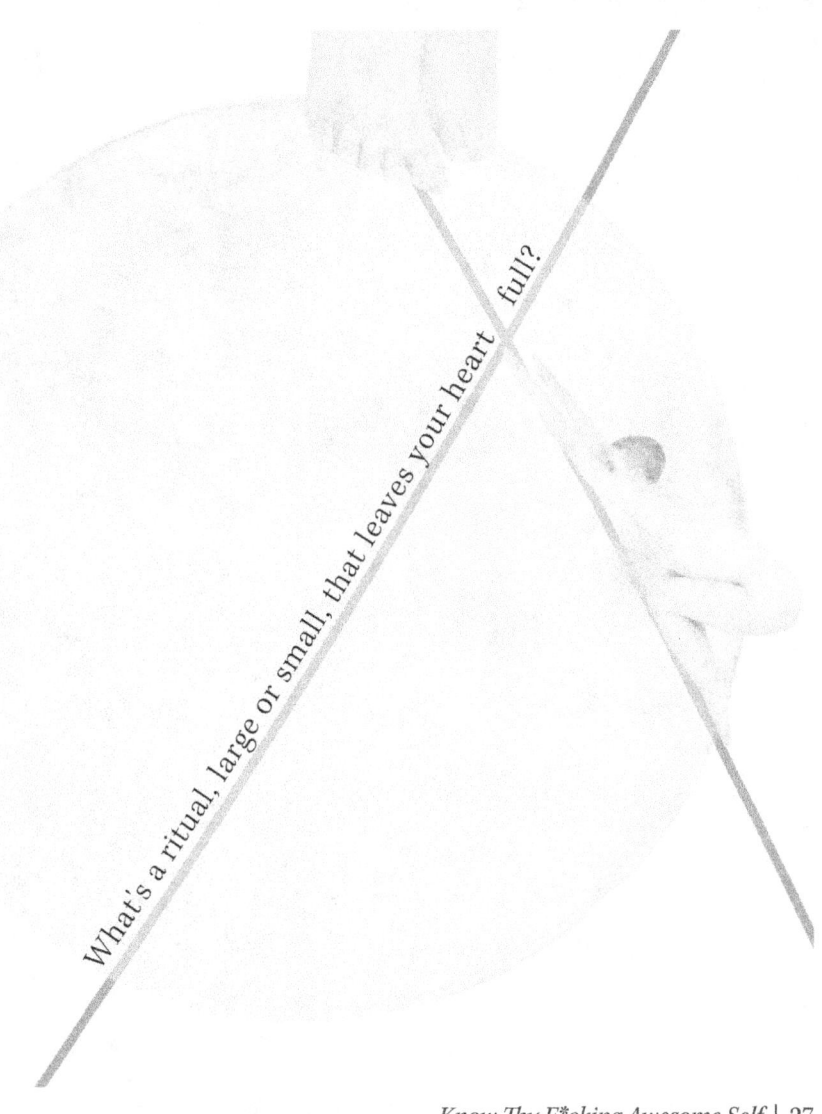

What's a ritual, large or small, that leaves your heart full?

When you feel yourself getting rigid, how do you bust out?

Who
helps
you
hold
your
dreams?

What's a cause you love supporting?

Who helps you keep your balance when life is wiggly?

If you had the right team,
what would you achieve?

Know Thy F*cking Awesome Self | 32

What's a relationship you dream of transforming?

What new idea
would you only want
to explore
alone?

What new idea
would you only want
to explore in a
group?

Know Thy F*cking Awesome Self | 34

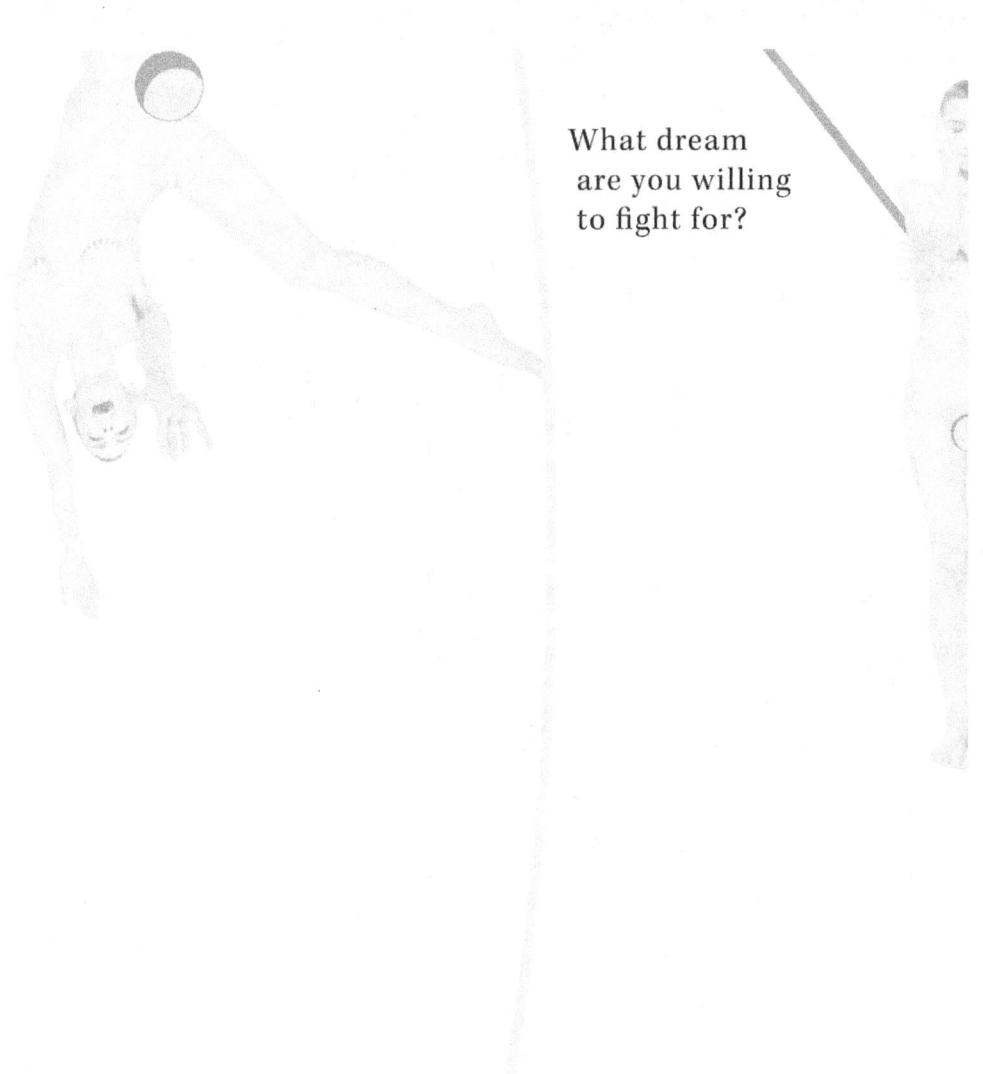

What dream are you willing to fight for?

What vision for humanity would you like to help create in the world?

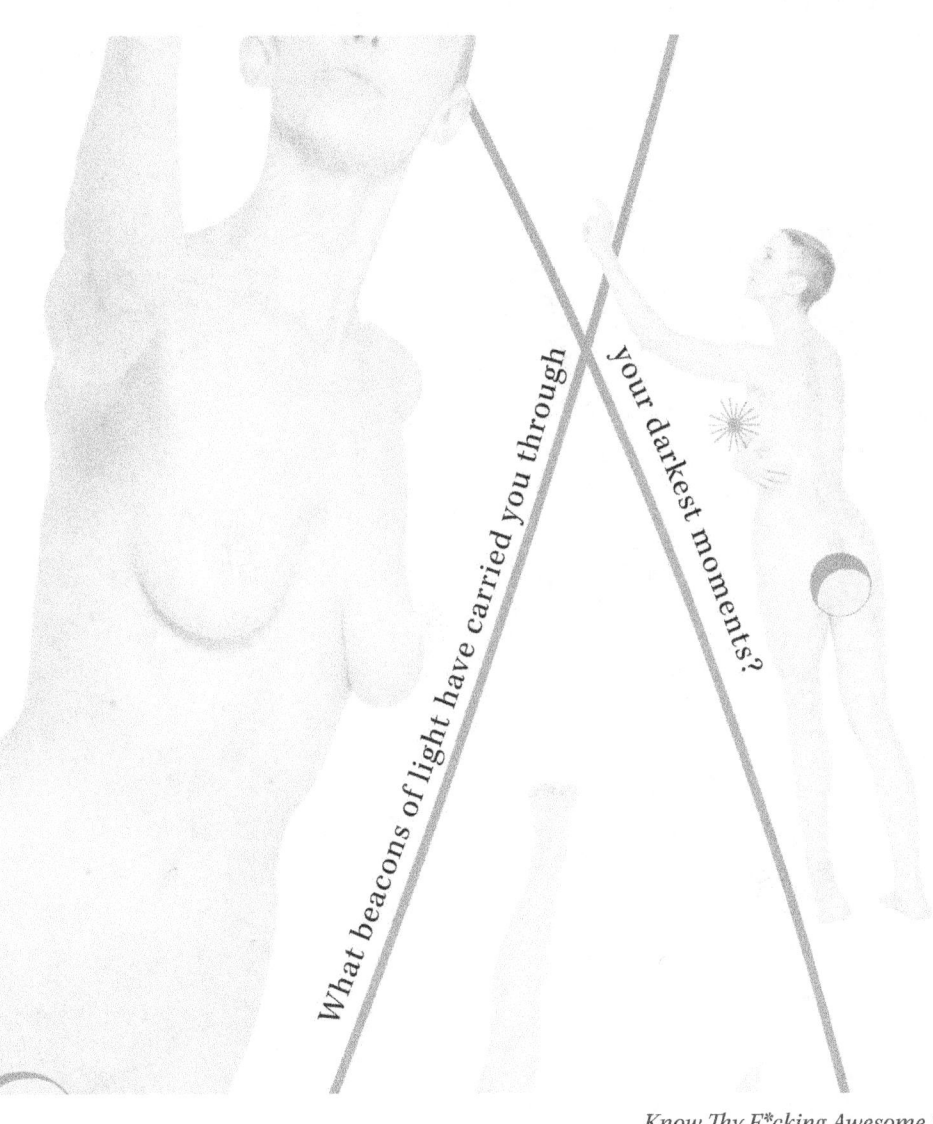

How do you want to transform your community?

What do you love about the ocean?

What do you love about the earth?

How has your tribe transformed you?

Where do you need more adventure?

Where do you need more structure?

How are expectations for justice and fairness communicated in the communities you are part of?

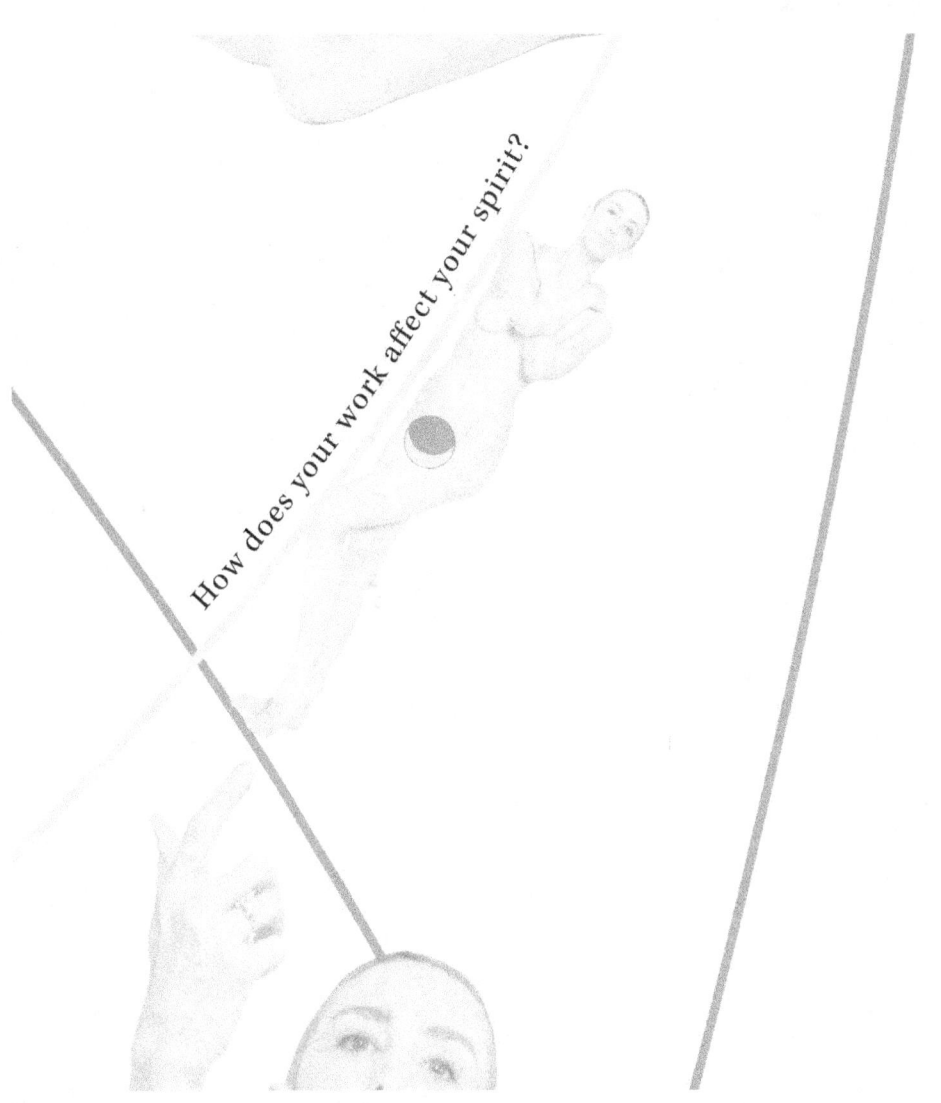

How does your work affect your spirit?

What new beauty can you create to electrify your network?

When do you lead with love?

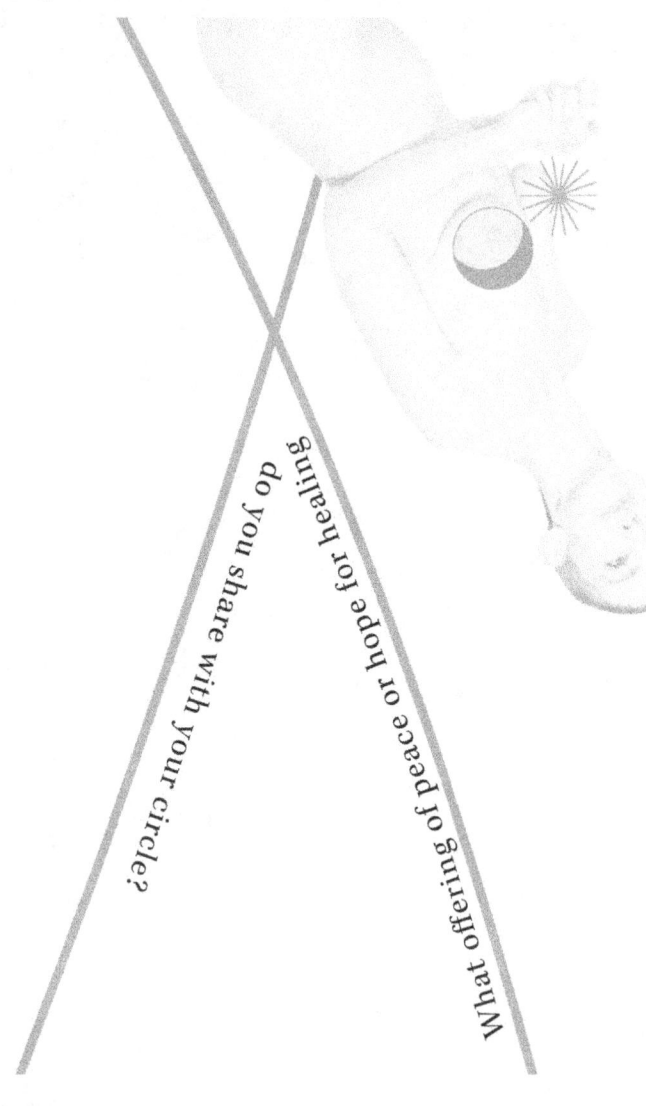

What offering of peace or hope for healing do you share with your circle?

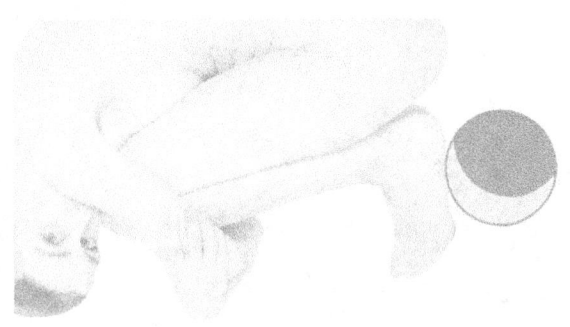

When do you love to feel silent in a crowd?

How do you get out of your head and into your body?

What would be a transcendent group experience for you?

When do you choose friendly?

When do you choose aloof?

How does sadness serve you?

How do you give generously of your self to others?

How do you practice compassion?

When you feel
deeply supported
by your friends,
family,
community,
and the world,
how
do
you
shine?

Know Thy F*cking Awesome Self | 54

When life as you know it has crumbled, how do you begin again?

What's something you've tried reluctantly and *loved?*

Pinpoint a moment you felt like a new *you*. Details?

When and how do you choose to step outside your comfort zone?

When do you meander?

When do you plunge in?

How do you invite, discuss and navigate ideas that are new-to-you or different from what you believe?

You have a day to spoil yourself. What do you do?

How do you stay connected to your community?

What dream are you ready to make real?

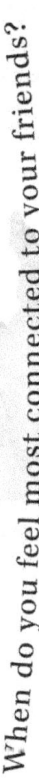

When do you feel most connected to your friends?

When and what do you love to sing?

After intense, hard work, what's your favorite way to relax?

Know Thy F*cking Awesome Self | 66

What silence stifles connection?

What is your idea of a perfect brunch?

What new idea are you ready to share?

What do you love most about your friends?

How are you reflected in your home?

How do you aim to inspire your community?

*Know Thy F*cking Awesome Self* | 72

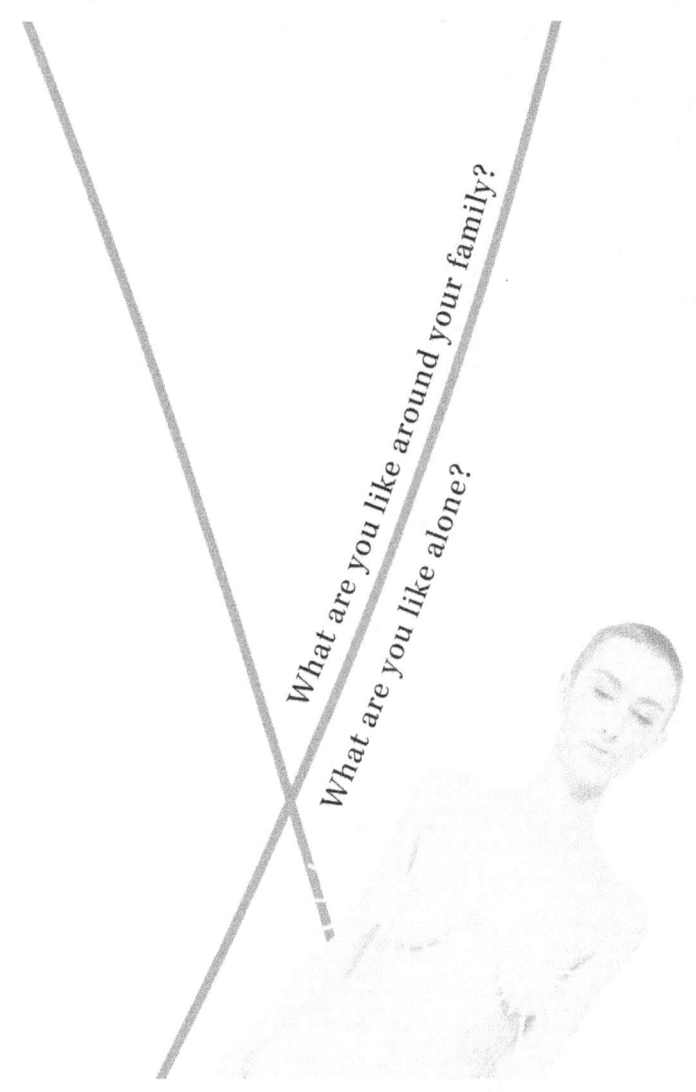

What are you like around your family?

What are you like alone?

When do you feel most inspired in your work?

What if you are the life of the party?

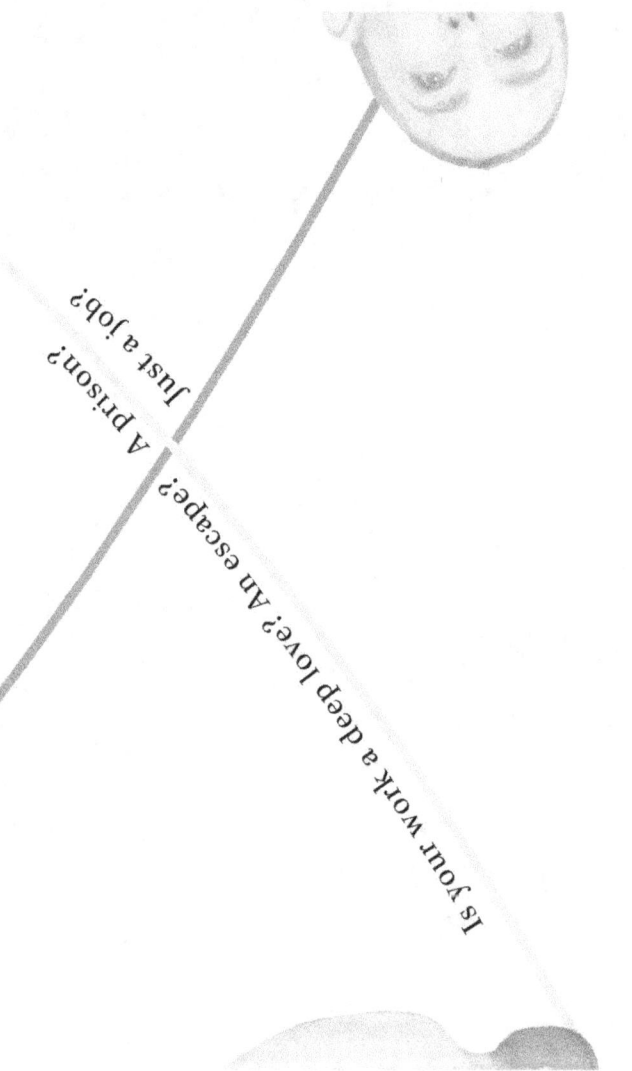

Is your work a deep love? An escape? A prison? Just a job?

When do you let yourself shine?

What's your go-to move for showing someone you care?

Know Thy F*cking Awesome Self | 78

When do the mean voices in your head stop you from sharing your heart?

What have you learned from leading a team?

What have you learned as part of a team?

What tiny, practical acts of love do you show yourself?

What innovative work inspires you?

How do you maintain a sense of self in a relationship?

How has your journey so far made you wise?

What
has the
influence
of friendship
inspired
that
you
would
never
have
attempted
solo?

What's a mountain you are climbing?

Who in your life helps or forces you to grow?

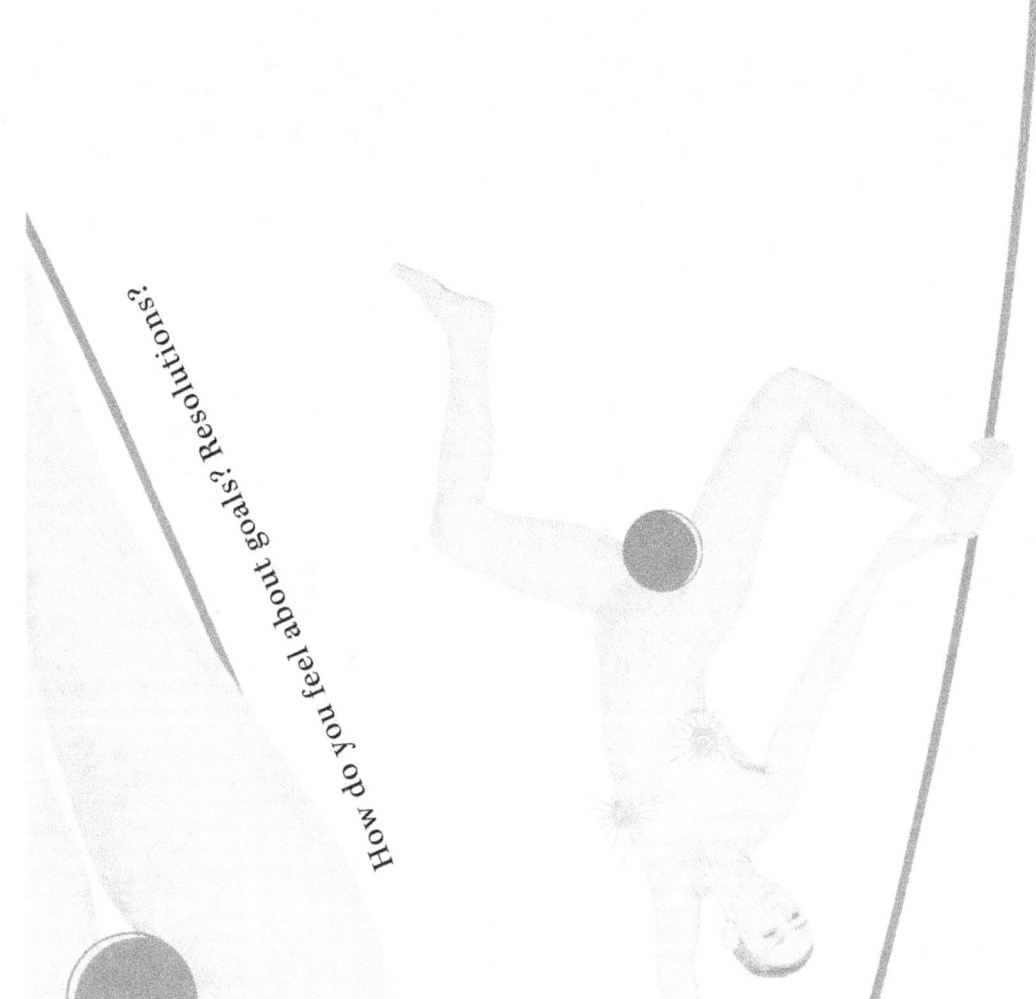

How do you feel about goals? Resolutions?

What does your armor look like? How does it protect?

What's the career leap never taken that keeps whispering?

What
do
you
love
about
failure?

Know Thy F*cking Awesome Self | 92

When do you feel free?

What are you determined to realize through your work?

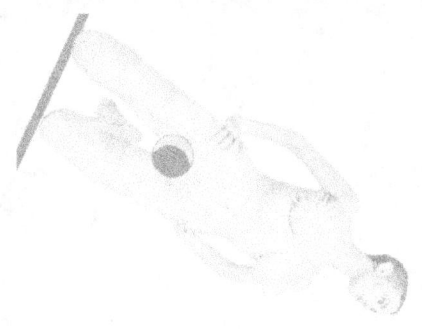

What does your most impulsive self teach you?

How do you protect your you-time?

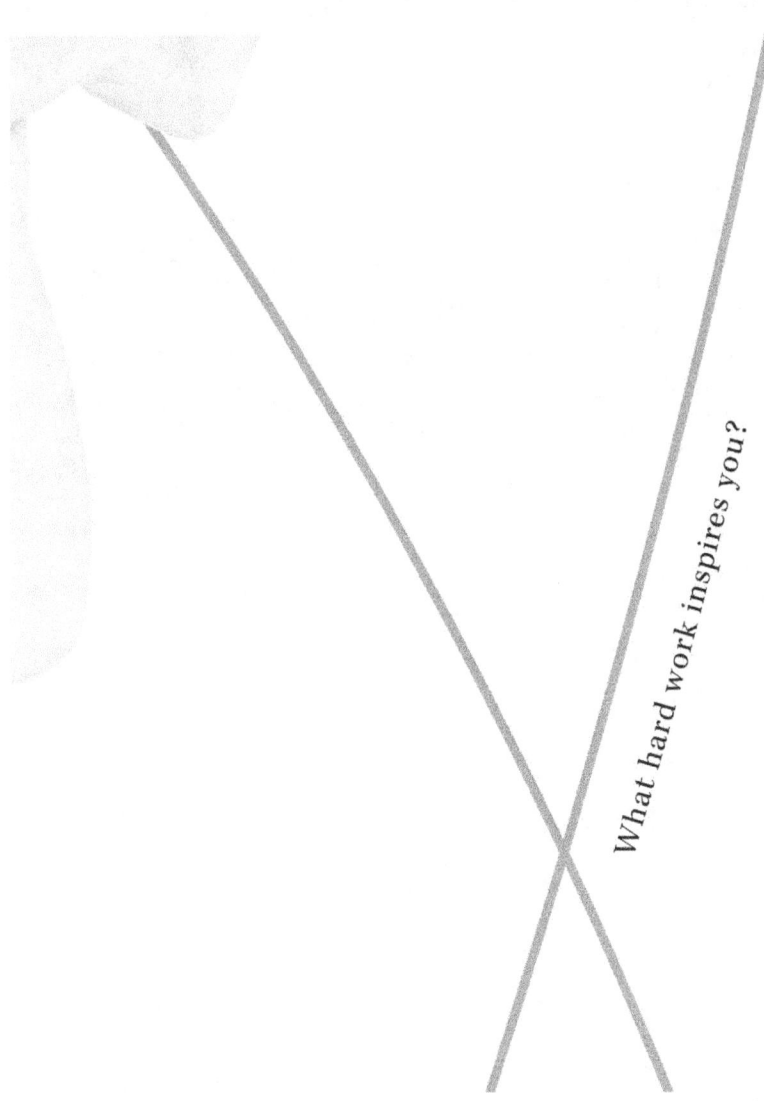

What hard work inspires you?

What beauty would you like to build?

As a leader, what's your best quality?

How do you feel about your responsibilities?

When do you prefer to brianstorm alone? In a group?

When the work is finished
how will you rest?

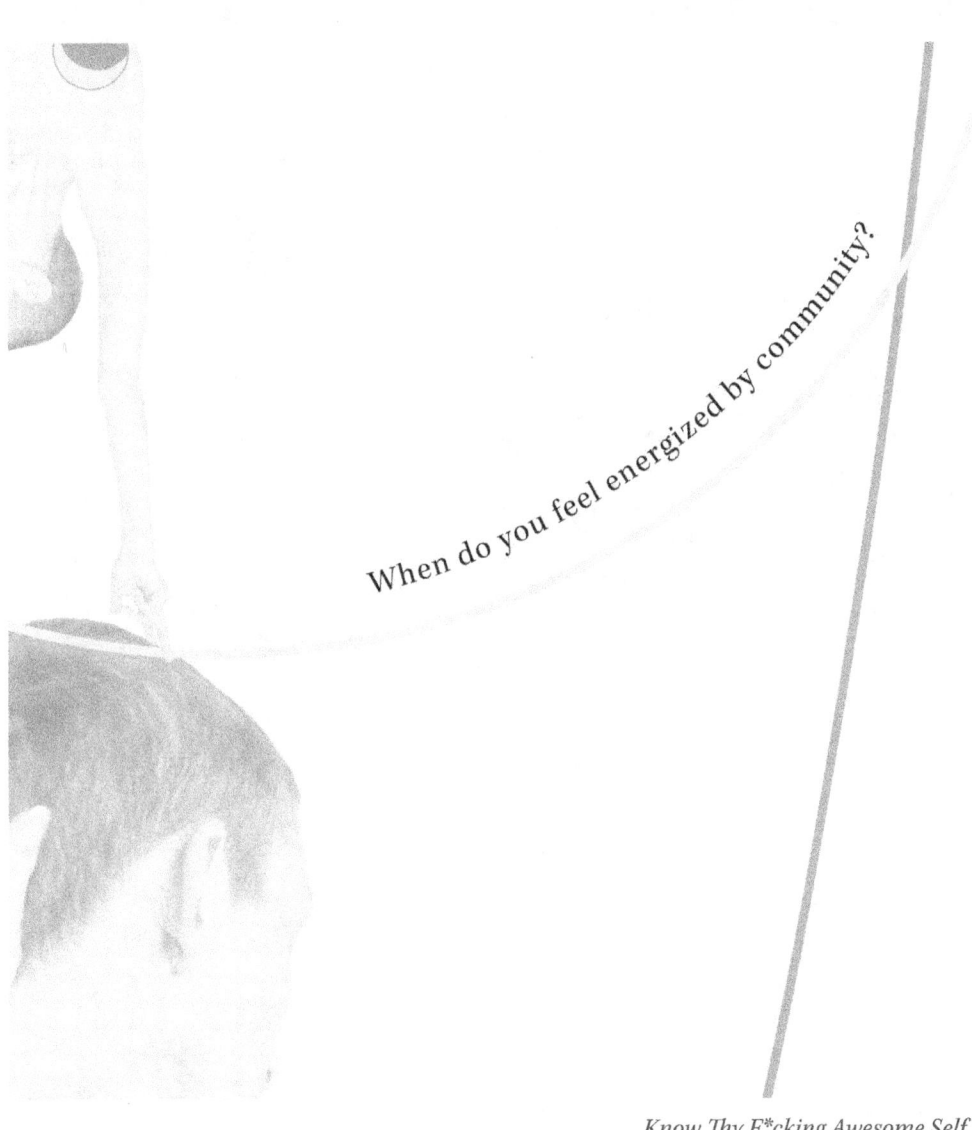

When do you feel energized by community?

How are you stuck?

Tell a story of being alone in a crowd and feeling connected.

When do you let yourself to break the rules?

When do you lead with feeling?

When do you feel proudest of your work?

When you are in a puddle of despair, what music lifts you out,

dries you off,
and
reignites your heart?

With whom do you celebrate your work?

What parts of yourself do you love, love, love?

How does your family cheer you up?

A new beginning calls to you. What is it?

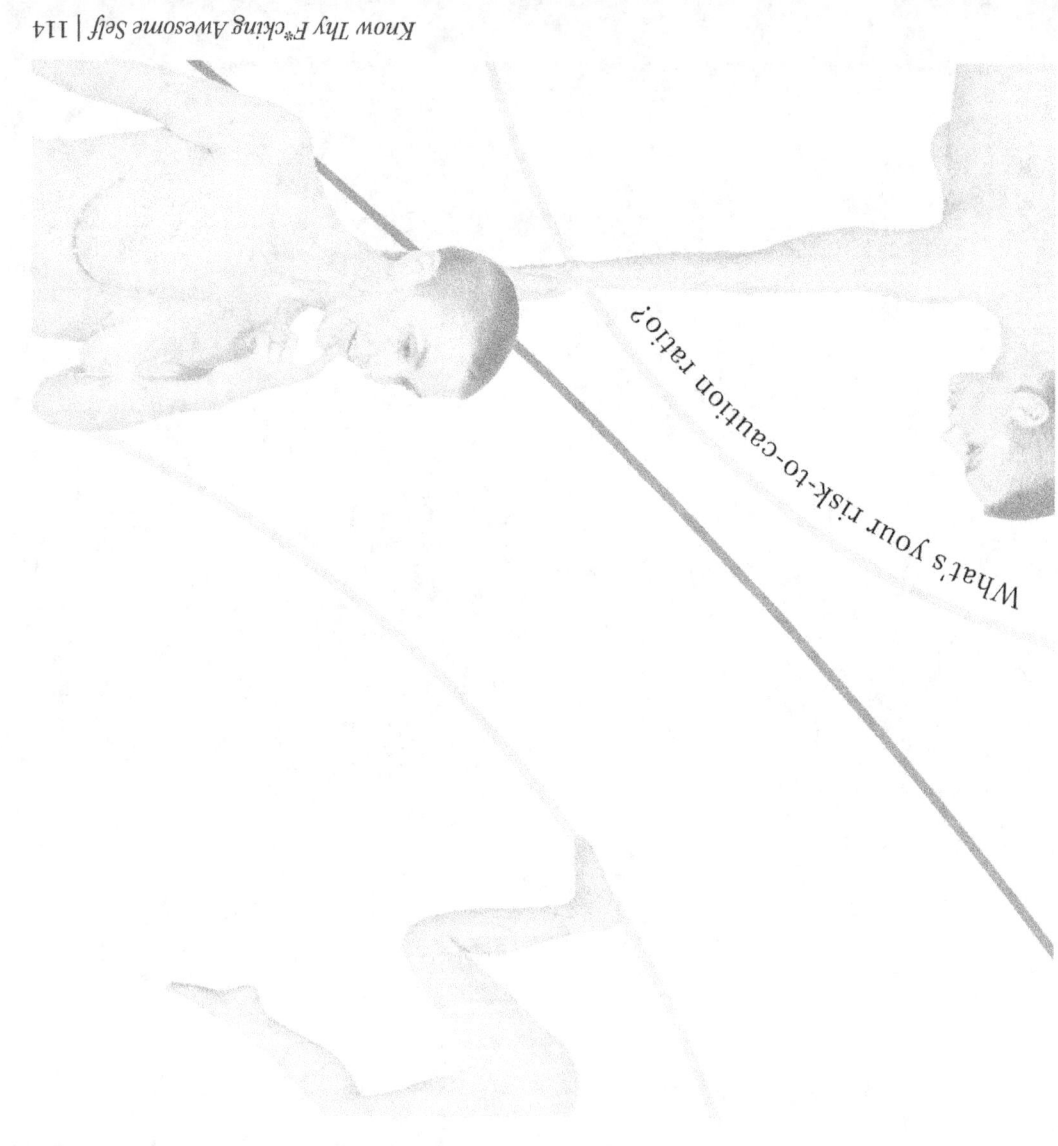

What's your risk-to-caution ratio?

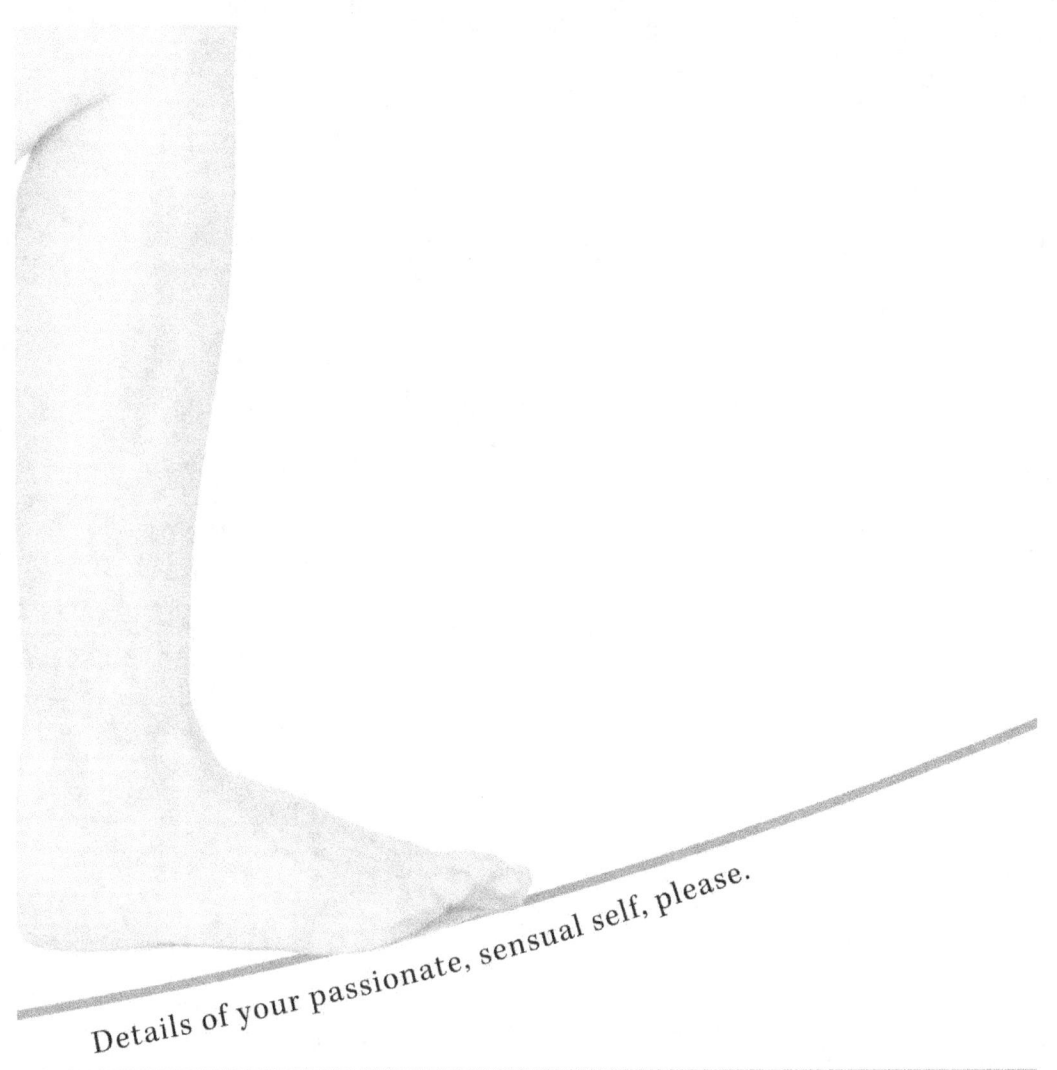

Details of your passionate, sensual self, please.

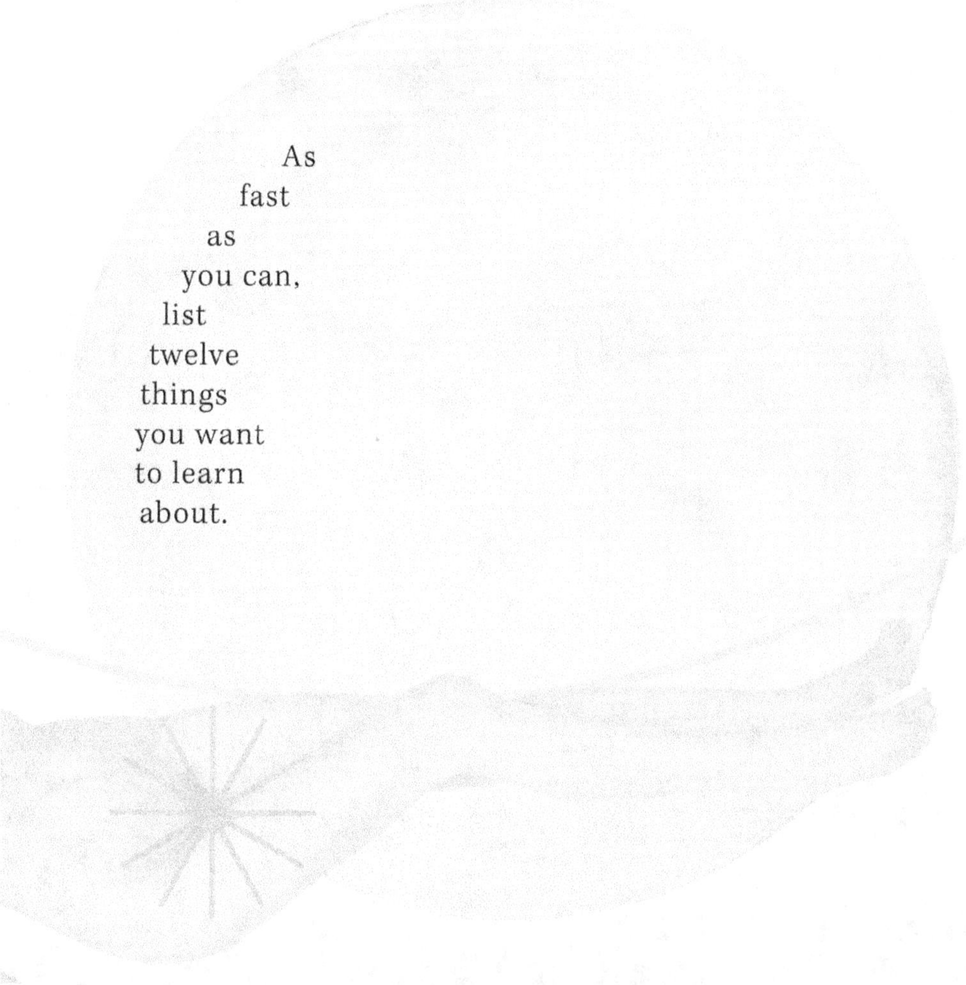

As
fast
as
you can,
list
twelve
things
you want
to learn
about.

Describe something you find deeply beautiful.

Who's your partner in curiosity?

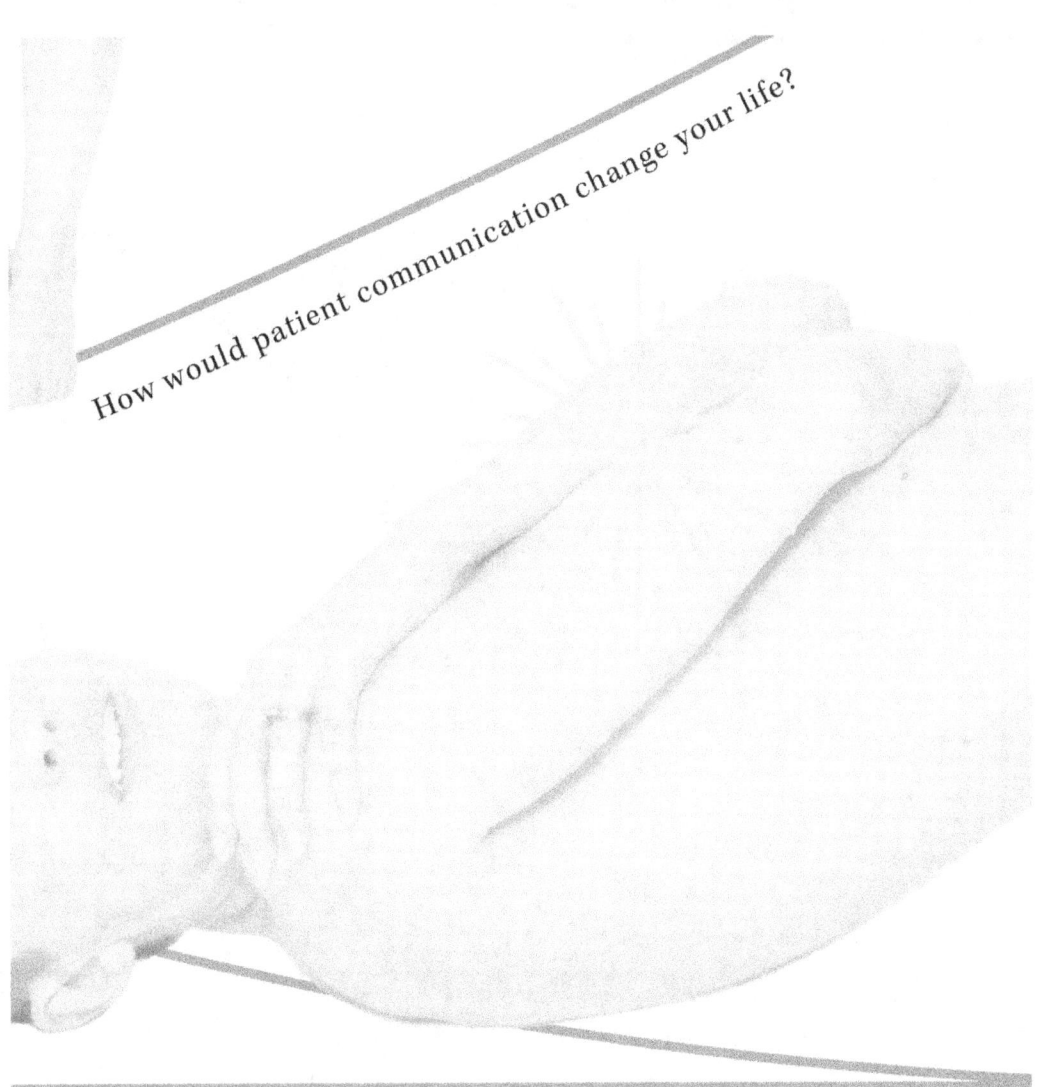

How would patient communication change your life?

Tell a story about exploring with your physical senses.

What are you currently learning?

When do you feel free in your body?

What do you wish you could communicate more clearly about yourself?

Share all the ways your desire manifests.

What do you wish your family would ask you about yourself?

What does your most impulsive self want *now*?

Know Thy F*cking Awesome Self | 126

If the world is your family, what role do you play?

What does the beginning of your next chapter hold?

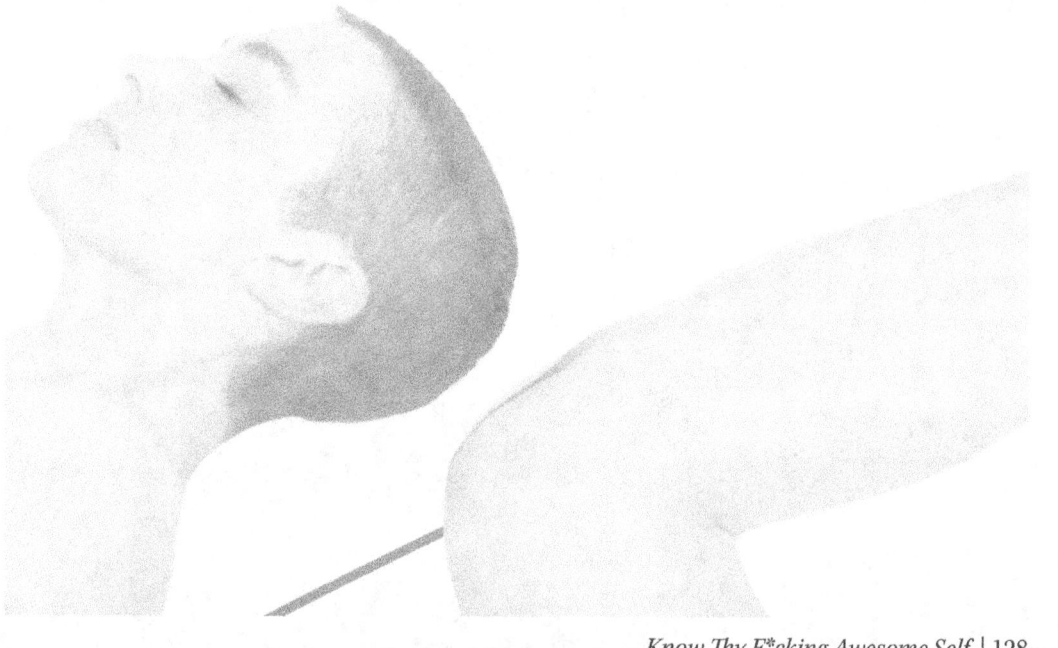

Know Thy F*cking Awesome Self | 128

When do you feel the most at home in your body?

Where do you dream of traveling next?

What part of yourself do you love to show off?

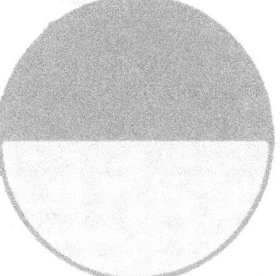

What's your version of spiritual exploration?

How do you embody beauty?

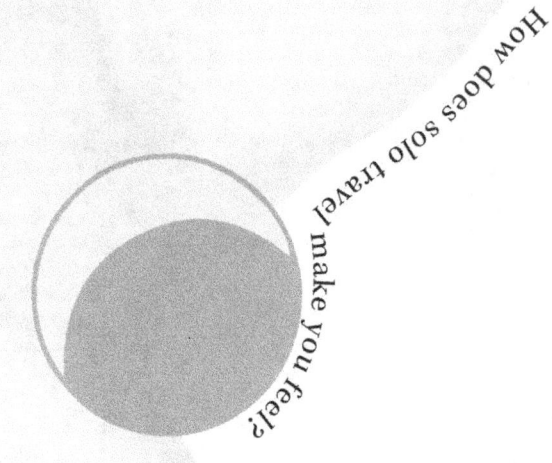

How does solo travel make you feel?

What self-care rituals do you nurture your body with?

When do you like to rile people up?

If your body is a temple,
what kind of temple is it?

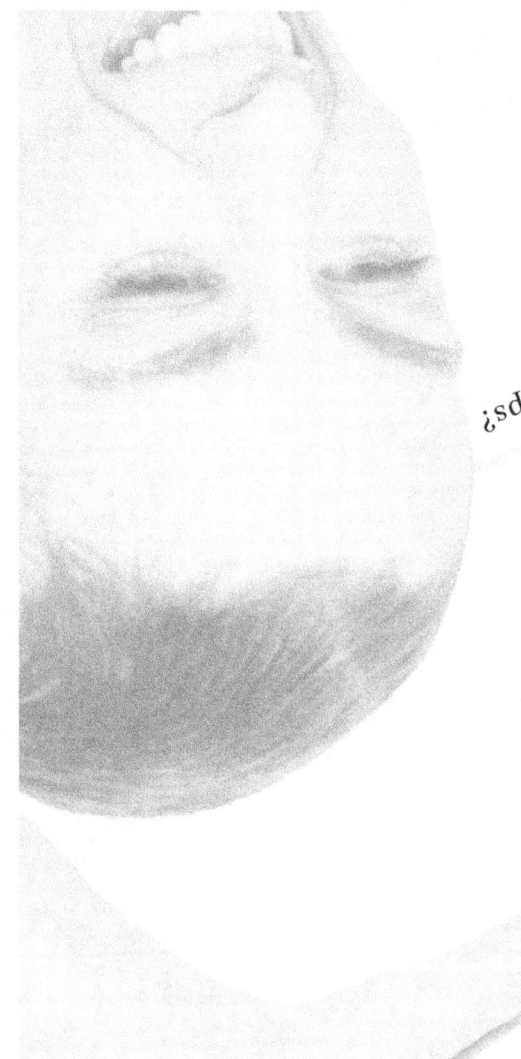

Where do you find freedom in groups?

How has judgment of your body shaped your being?

What new hopes do you have for your career?

Know Thy F*cking Awesome Self | 140

How does the touch of a loved one affect your balance?

What responsibility are you ready to set down?

When or where do you delight in the deepeest darkness?

What needs expansion in your life right now?

When do you feel rich?

How does your not enough-ness lead to an overwhelm of too much-ness?

When does beauty give you hope?

When
do you
prefer implicit
communication?

When
do you
prefer
explicit
communication?

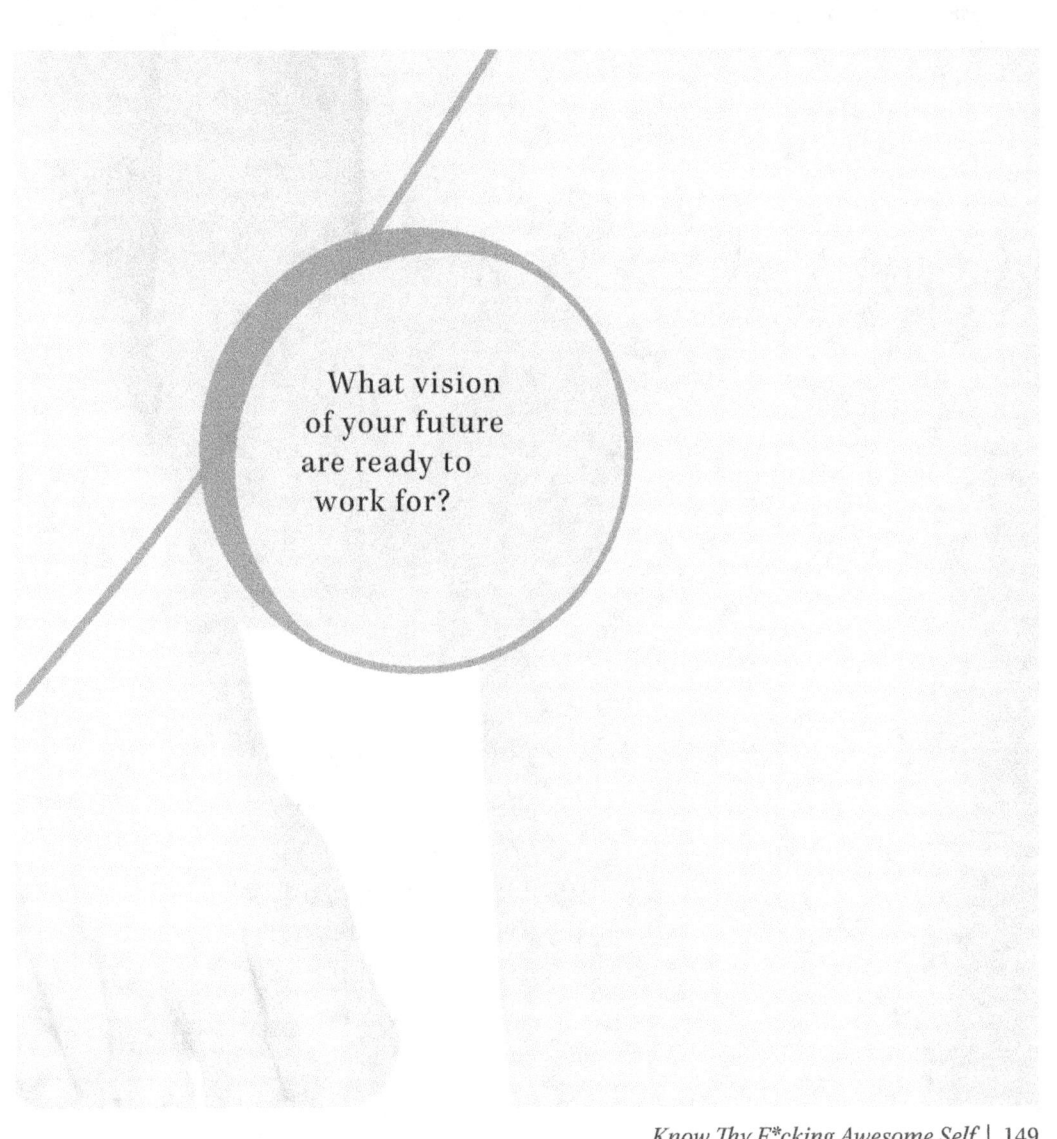

If if the
answer to one of
life's mysteries could
be revealed to you,
what would you
want to know?

You are now required to be "lazy" for two hours a day.

How will you spend them?

Who do you want to say a big YES to right now?

What do you value about the work you do in the world?

When do optimistic words hurt more than they help?

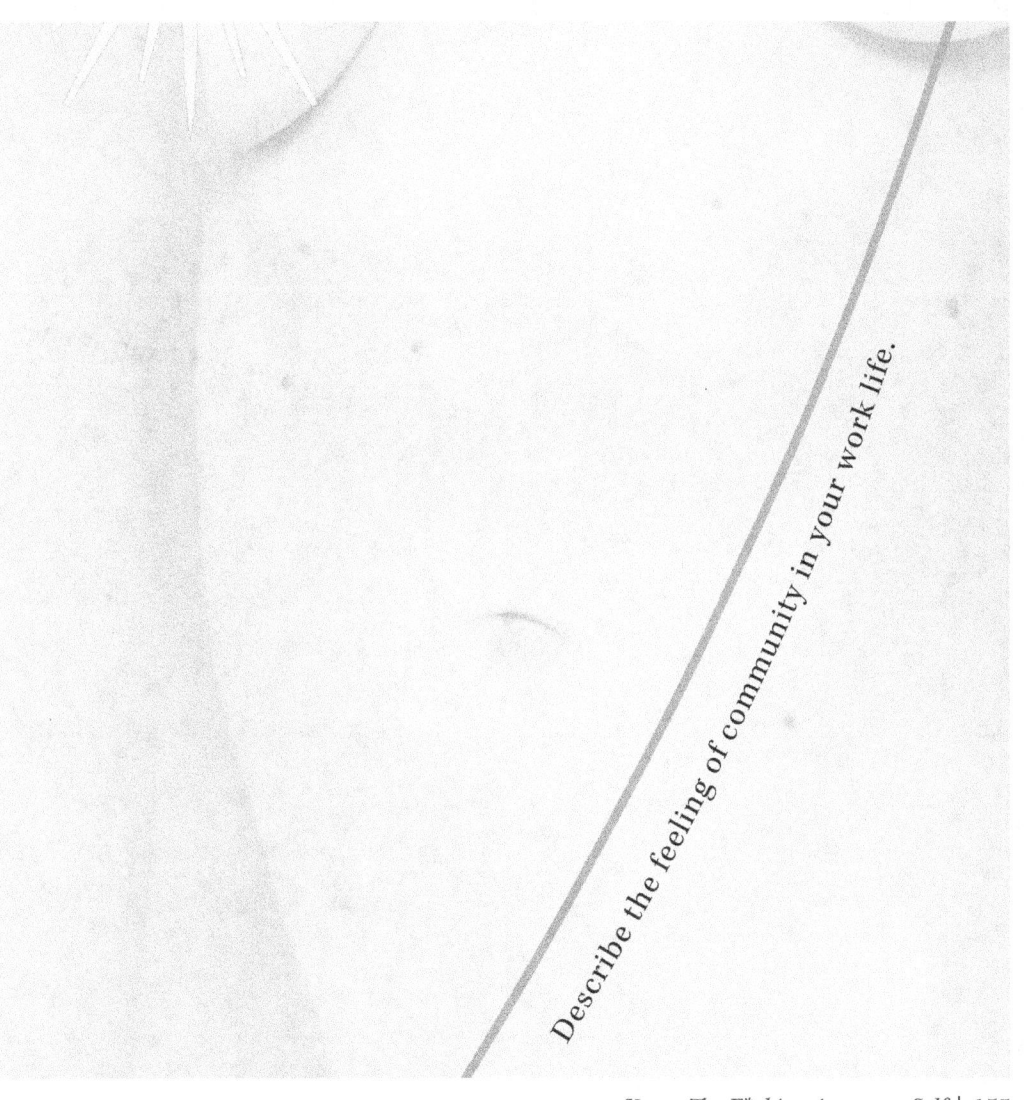

Describe the feeling of community in your work life.

What have you learned lately that's leveled up your lifestyle?

Describe your ultimate sensual group experience.

What does the conversation between your inner anxious perfectionist and optimistic adventurer sound like?

Know Thy F*cking Awesome Self | 158

Where do you see beauty in humanity?

How do you turn your inner editor off so you can create wildly?

Know Thy F*cking Awesome Self | 160

Notice three feelings most alive in you right now.

Where are they in your body?

Share a story of generosity.

How do you let your body know it is loved?

What new self expression is it time to explore?

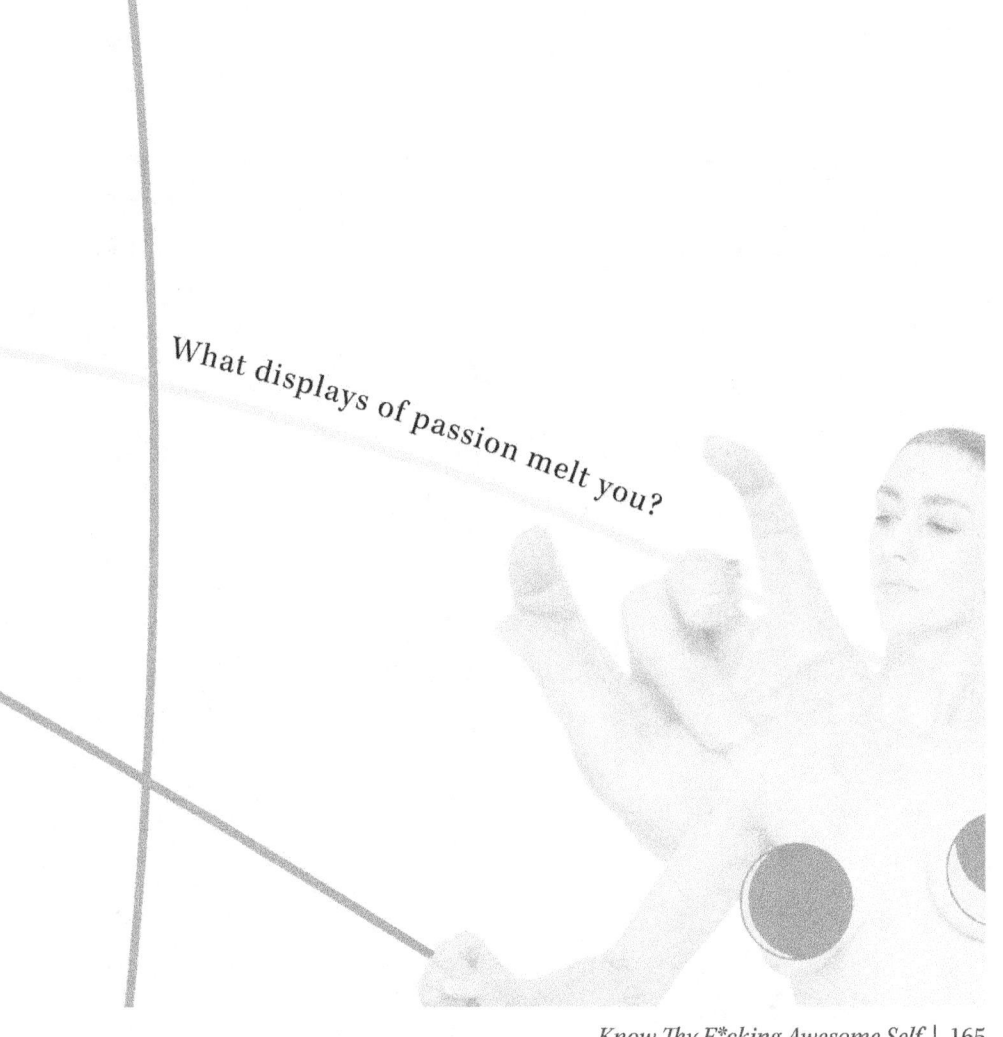

What displays of passion melt you?

If the whole world felt like your family, how would you live differently?

Where is your intuition? Head? Heart? Spirit?

Know Thy F*cking Awesome Self

How does your family inspire you?

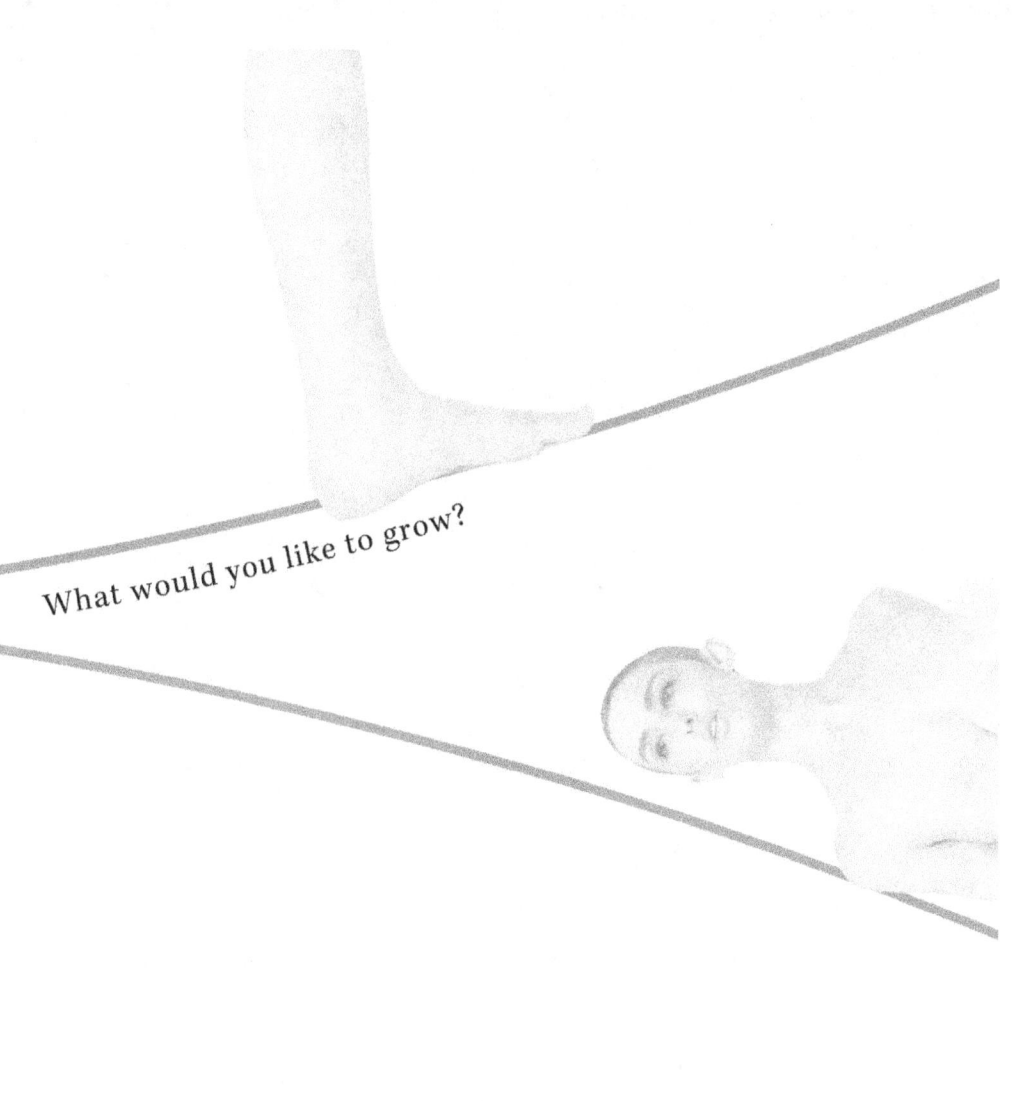

What would you like to grow?

What are you rebuilding?

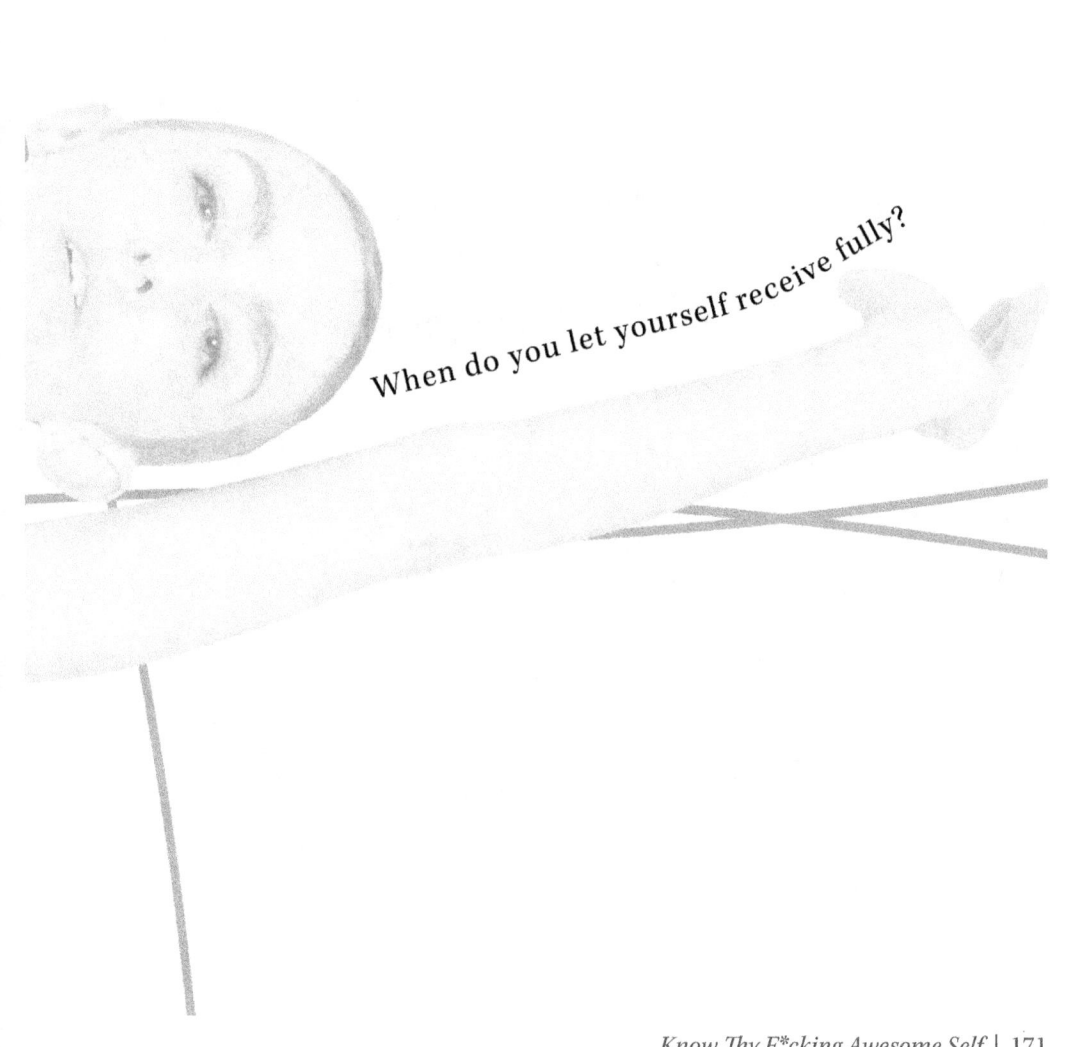

When do you let yourself receive fully?

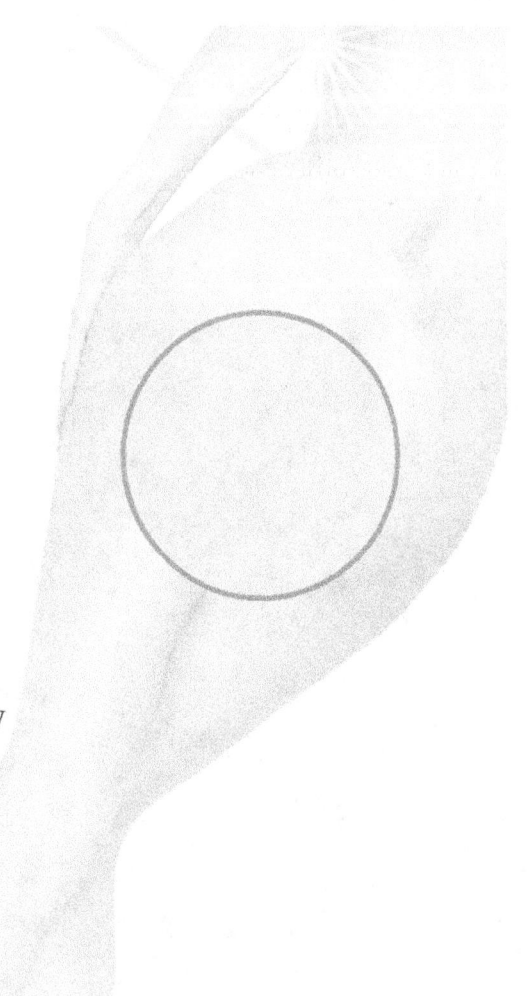

Tell the story
of a time
curiosity
ended
a fight.

What is your perfect day of hedonism?

Tell the story of a time jealousy ruined a connection.

What's
your
body
asking
for
right
now?

Describe a deeply sensual experience you crave.

Know Thy F*cking Awesome Self | 176

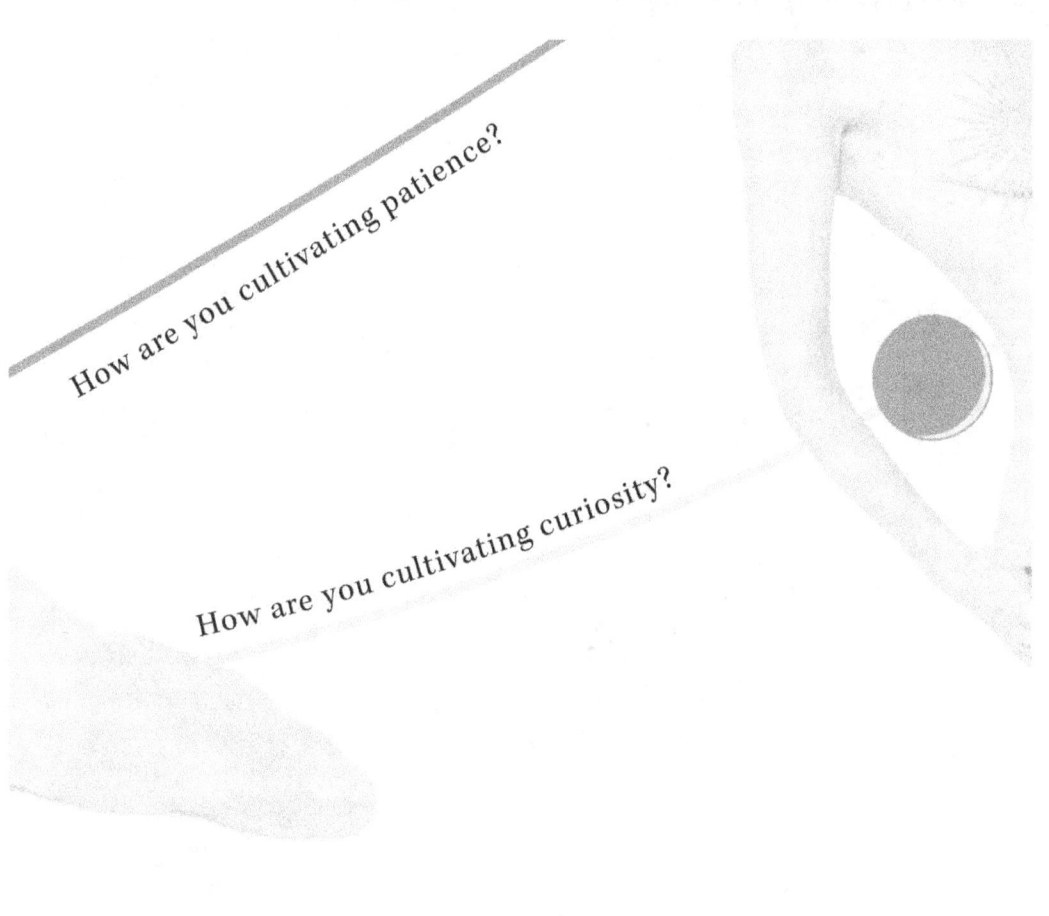

How are you cultivating patience?

How are you cultivating curiosity?

How have your ideas of pleasure evolved?

Know Thy F*cking Awesome Self | 178

How does your family talk about physical pleasure?

What burning ground are you

crossing?

Know Thy F*cking Awesome Self | 180

What pleasure do you wish all of humanity could experience exactly as you do?

How are you a love warrior?

Tell a story of holidng a boundary firmly in place and feeling *satisfied*.

Tell the story of a tiny spark that began an inextinguishable transformation.

When has generosity yielded great pleasure?

Soul. How do you understand this word?

How does your body express creativity?

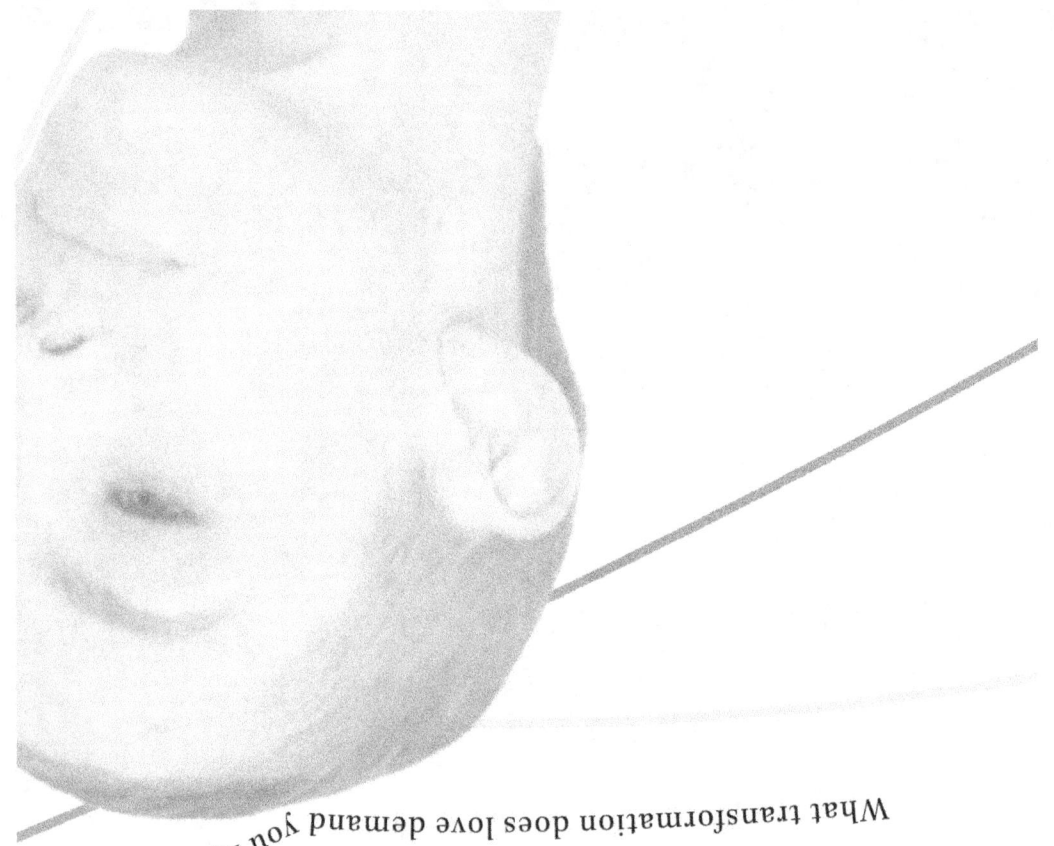

What transformation does love demand you fight for?

What do you do to replenish yourself?

Your nerves are jangly, all you want is solitude... but that's not an option. What do you do?

How would you like to refine your communication?

During times of deep despair, who is your support network?

How easily do you share your opinions with others?

What heavy burden are you ready to share?

What does a connected, balanced relationship look like?

When has restraint felt delicious?

When and how do you allow a connection to deepen?

When do you get feisty?

> What light-hearted messages are you bearing? What dark-hearted messages need releasing?

What battle have you emerged from, triumphant?

If you get curious about your despair, what do you discover?

What
cringey personal
shame spiral do
you still fall
into?

Where do you need to focus?

Where do you need to explore?

What are you wrestling with?

Know Thy F*cking Awesome Self | 204

What does the bridge between your optimism and pragmatism look like?

Who would you like to have a deep conversation with?

When do you feel most connected in your work?

Tell the story of forging deep connection with a trustowrthy friend.

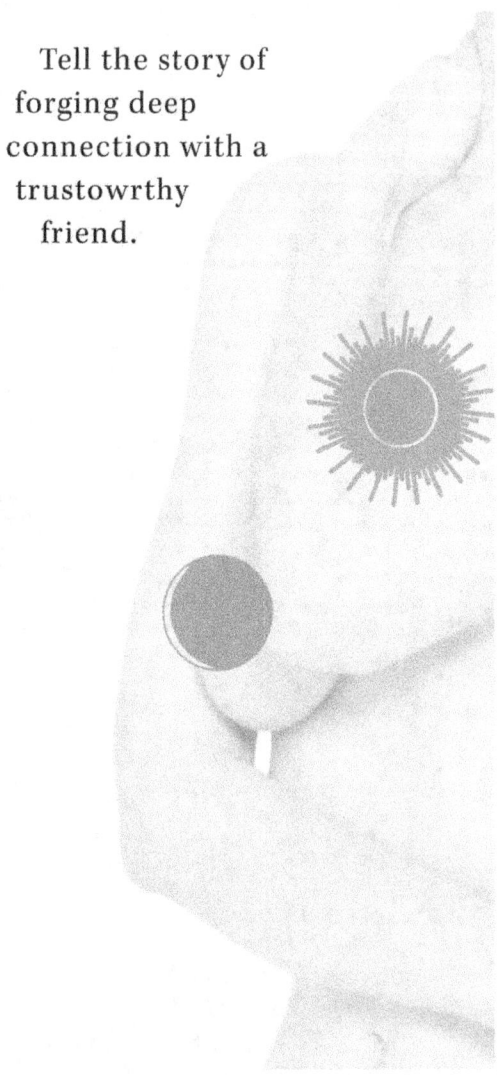

What would you like the world to know about the work you do in it?

How do
you honor
your
loved
ones
who have
gone on
to the
next
realm?

*Know Thy F*cking Awesome Self* | 210

What connection do you seek in friendship?

What's
your
favorite
way to
trick
someone?

What's
your
favorite
way to
treat
someone?

Know Thy F*cking Awesome Self | 212

How do you communicate with the people you love?

Tell the story of a project you struggled with, didn't give up on, and feel proud of.

What do you do when feelings are too great for words?

What everyday armor protects you?

How do you commune with the divine?

Know Thy F*cking Awesome Self | 217

Tell
the story
of a time
you were
deeply afraid
and how
it has
shaped
your
heart.

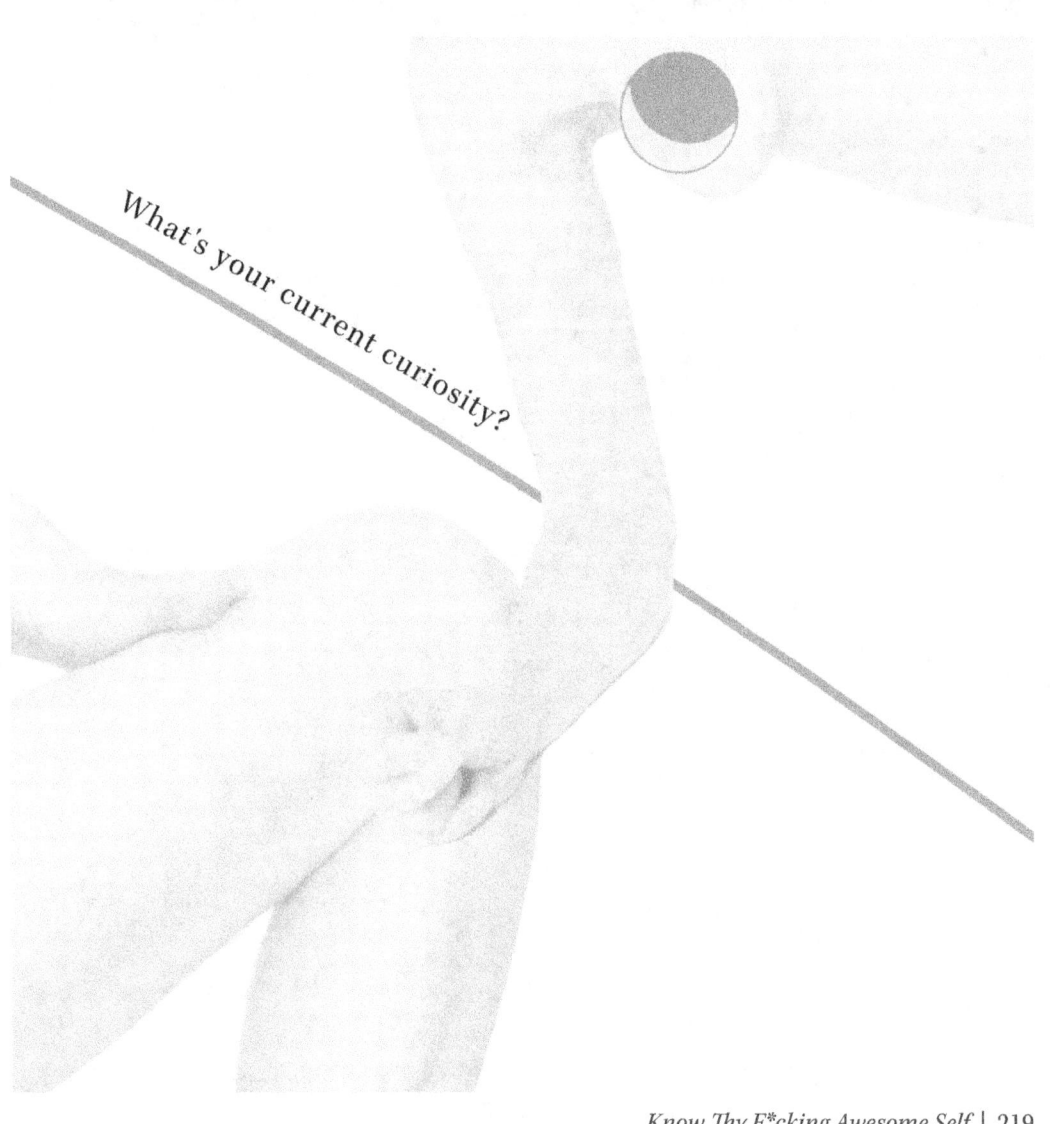

How do you share the ongoing battles in or with your family?

Tell the story of a burning question.

What do you understand about your sensitive parts?

How do you connect your mind and body?

What's something you've been curious about,

but are only now ready to tackle?

*Know Thy F*cking Awesome Self* | 224

What parts of your body are you still getting to know?

What hard questions have you been avoiding?

What have you learned with your fingers?

Tell the story of a time you went deep down the research rabbit hole.

When your thoughts are loud, how do you ground yourself?

How do you like to touch yourself?

How do you satisfy extreme curiosity?

How does touch from a loved one ground you?

Tell the story of a time you were glad you asked the question.

What new pleasure would you like to explore?

Who will you invite to join you?

Know Thy F*cking Awesome Self | 234

How do you feel about the way your family communicates?

When have you felt brave and broken-hearted?

What would you like to know about your family, but have never asked?

When did you dare to love, in spite of yourself?

What would you like to know about your self, but have never asked?

What imbalance are you ready to release?

Know Thy F*cking Awesome Self | 240

Tell the story of speaking corgagoues words.

Who in your life is an ocean of love?

How do you play responsibly?

How do you make, find or contribute to peace?

The world can be jangly.

Where do you need to be less responsible?

When does
breaking the
rules feel
awesome?

Know Thy F*cking Awesome Self | 246

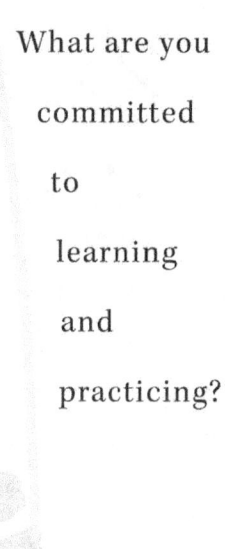

What are you

committed

to

learning

and

practicing?

What needs a revamp in your work life?

What relationship in your life wants a good conversation?

How do you decide when a relationship deserves commitment?

When and
to whom
do you
send
letters
in the
mail?

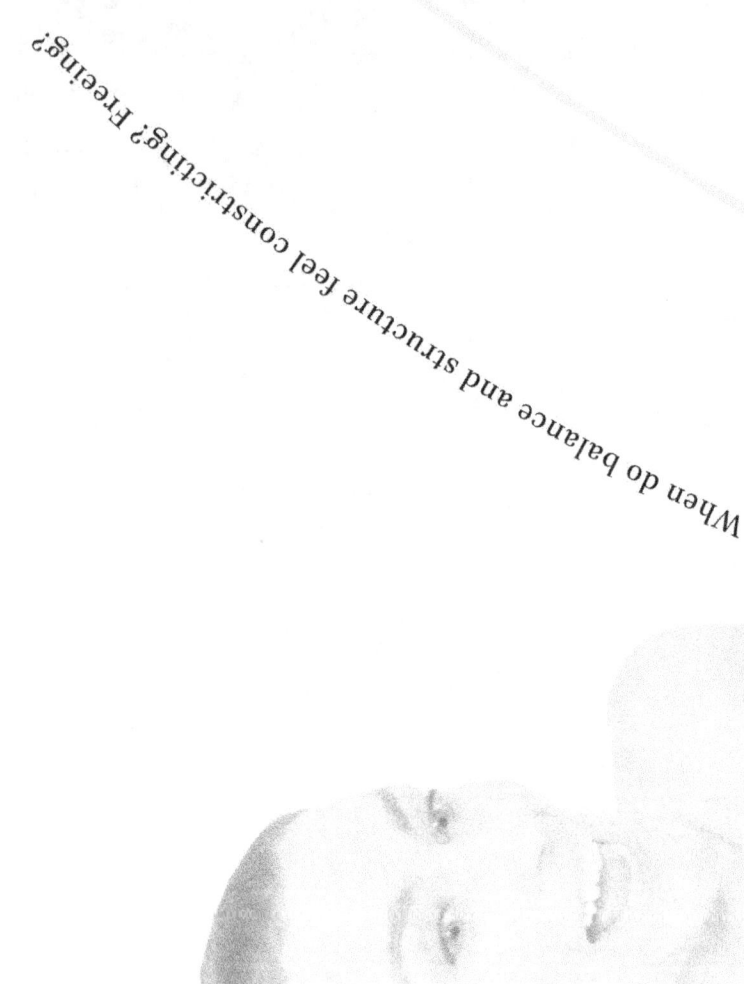

When do balance and structure feel constricting? Freeing?

When big feelings take over, where do you seek refuge?

Who inspires you to treat others with integrity?

What does "home" feel like?

Tell the story of a difficult decision you finally made.

What have you learned about adventure from your family?

When Life's Chasm of Hard Things tries to swallow you, who is your lifeline?

When you are home, what trip do you dream of?

When you are traveling, what visions of home return to you again and again?

Who is your secret keeper?

What familial wisdom have you inherited?

Who are the love(r)s of your life?

How are
themes of
motherhood
and
fatherhood
present
in
your
life?

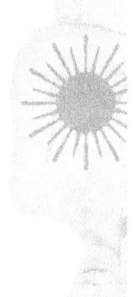

How did you meet your best friend?

Who is your chosen family?

When you notice your own personal growth, with whom do you share it?

When you feel most alone, how do you find your way back to belonging?

It's time to weed your relationship garden.
What must go?

How does your family handle big feelings?

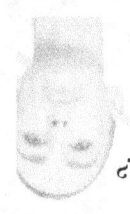

When you feel insecure and afraid, who steadies you?

When do you feel cozy, quiet and loved?

How do you play with your beloved?

Know Thy F*cking Awesome Self | 272

What have you been defending that you are ready to surrender?

Who do you love to nurture?

What is your perfect day of hedonism?

You aren't related, but you're family. How did you choose each other?

What are your nurturing impulses?

What do you know about navigating conflict with people you love?

With whom do you wish to share the fruits of your labor?

What do you
notice about how you
express yourself in
person?
On the phone?
In a text?
Message?
Email?
Snail mail?

Describe
your
belly
as an
ally
of your
sensuality.

What question are you burning to ask a certain someone?

Will you please write your body a love poem?

How do you practice sharing feelings with a partner?

How do you use words to defend yourself?

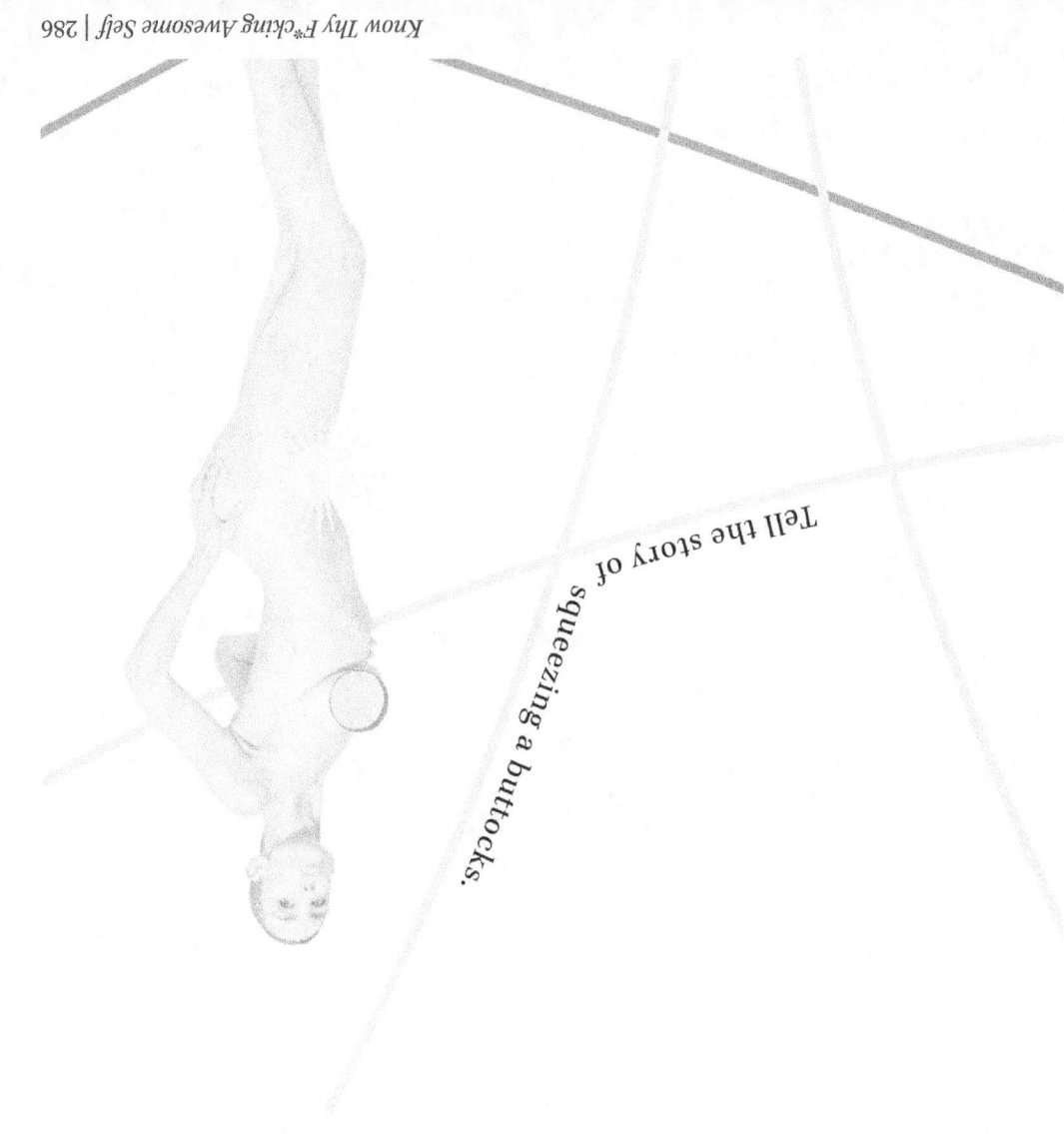

Tell the story of squeezing a buttocks.

What painful words still echo in your heart?

How do you love to share your sensuality with a partner?

What is the recipe for a nourishing hug?

Who

celebrates

you?

Know Thy F*cking Awesome Self | 290

What are you hungry for? How do you want to be fed?

What new idea are you ready to tend?

Know Thy F*cking Awesome Self | 292

How do you

play your way

out of grumpiness?

What part of your daily routine are you ready to let go of?

How does your individual self fit into your family group?

On those days when you feel too blurry to function,

how do you make your way back to clarity?

Know Thy F*cking Awesome Self | 296

Where in your home does creativity live?

What little, practical acts of love make you swoon?

What is your sick day comfort food?

Tell a story of finding nourishment or healing in a gathering:

Tell a story of feeling not good enough in a group.

What is your heartbreak comfort food?

What triggers your most rigid, controlling impulses?

Where does your household feel balanced?

When do you feel most grounded?

What did you learn about fighting from your family?

What's something you want to learn to make?

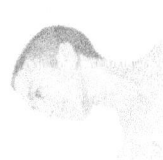

What in your home needs transformation?

What ritual gives you hope?

When does your home feel like a prison?
When does it feel like an escape?

How do you undervalue yourself?

When do you feel too crabby for optimism?

What attention does your sensual self need?

What would make your home feel more expansive?

When deep in struggle, who has your back?

Tell the story of a sunrise you loved.

Who are your personal advisors?

How do you play at work?

Who

gives

you

permission

to

be

a

mess?

Know Thy F*cking Awesome Self | 320

What are the weird parts of yourself you love?

Know Thy F*cking Awesome Self | 321

How do you handle perfectionism?

What do you love creating with a group?

What do you love creating alone?

What
stressor
does your
grownup self
need to address
so you can
move on?

Know Thy F*cking Awesome Self | 324

How does silence inspire you?

What part of your creativity would feel nourishing to practice?

What is your artist heart silently begging you to initiate?

Who's
an
artist
you
adore?

Playing Truth or Dare, what truth would you secretly want to be asked?

*Know Thy F*cking Awesome Self*

How has ritual or tradition shaped your life?

What's something you would be excited to do, but only as a dare?

What
critique
from a
loved one
has stayed
with
you?

When do you feel radiant, daring and strong?

What words of devotion connect you to others?

Know Thy F*cking Awesome Self | 334

When are you courageously patient?

What words do you need to hear to heal?

Share a story of feeling utterly beautiful.

What words are the weapons of your inner critic?

How might you express your desire for connection more clearly?

Where do you find pleasure in your daily work?

Tell the story of a time you had the courage to know and be known.

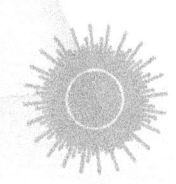

How do you calm your nervous system?

How do you talk to people when you're grumpy?

What new pleasure practice deserves your devotion?

Know Thy F*cking Awesome Self | 344

What role do you play in your family?

When the jaws of "not good enough" begin to bite, what do you do?

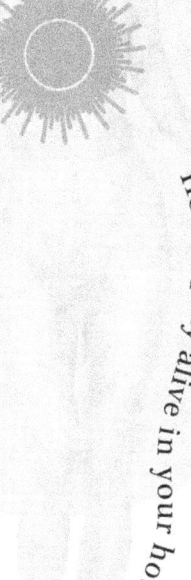

How is play alive in your household?

What are you reaping?
What did you sow?

When do you feel like your brightest, shiniest, most on-fire lit up self?

How have pain and sadness evolved you?

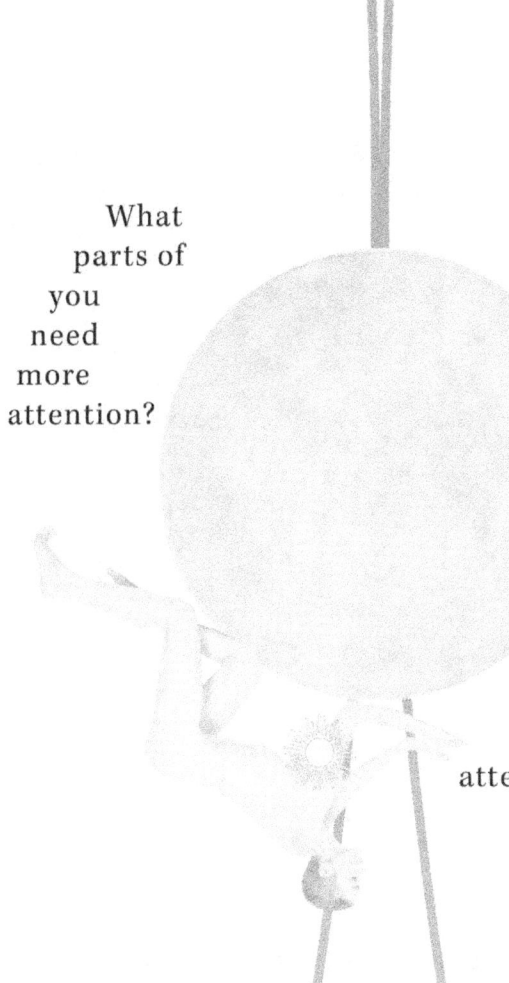

What
parts of
you
need
more
attention?

What
parts
of you
need
to pay
more
attention?

What lyric or line is a balm for you?

Know Thy F*cking Awesome Self | 352

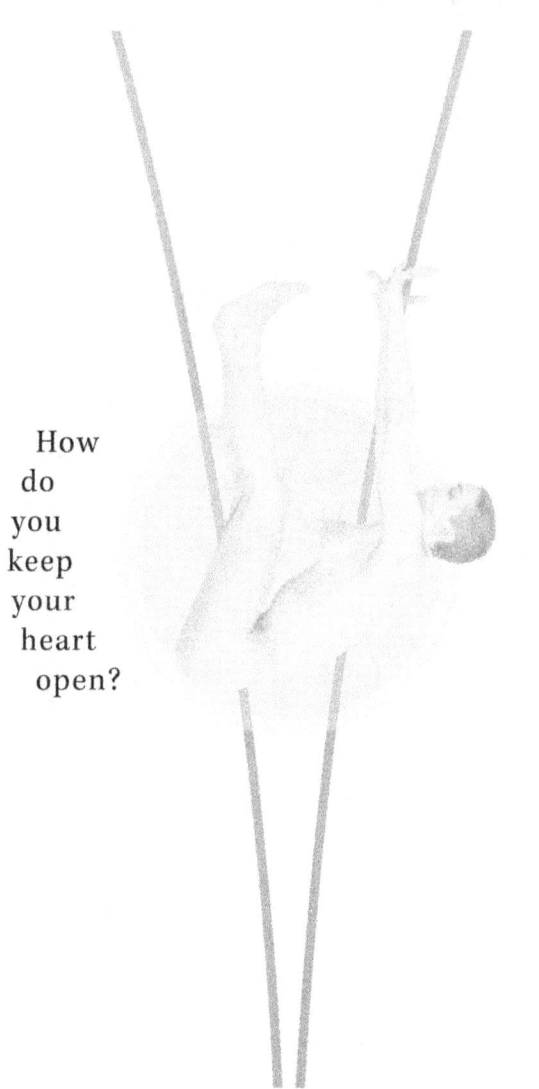

How
do
you
keep
your
heart
open?

What
are
the
joys
of
playing
alone?

What
are
the
joys
of
playing
with
others?

Know Thy F*cking Awesome Self | 354

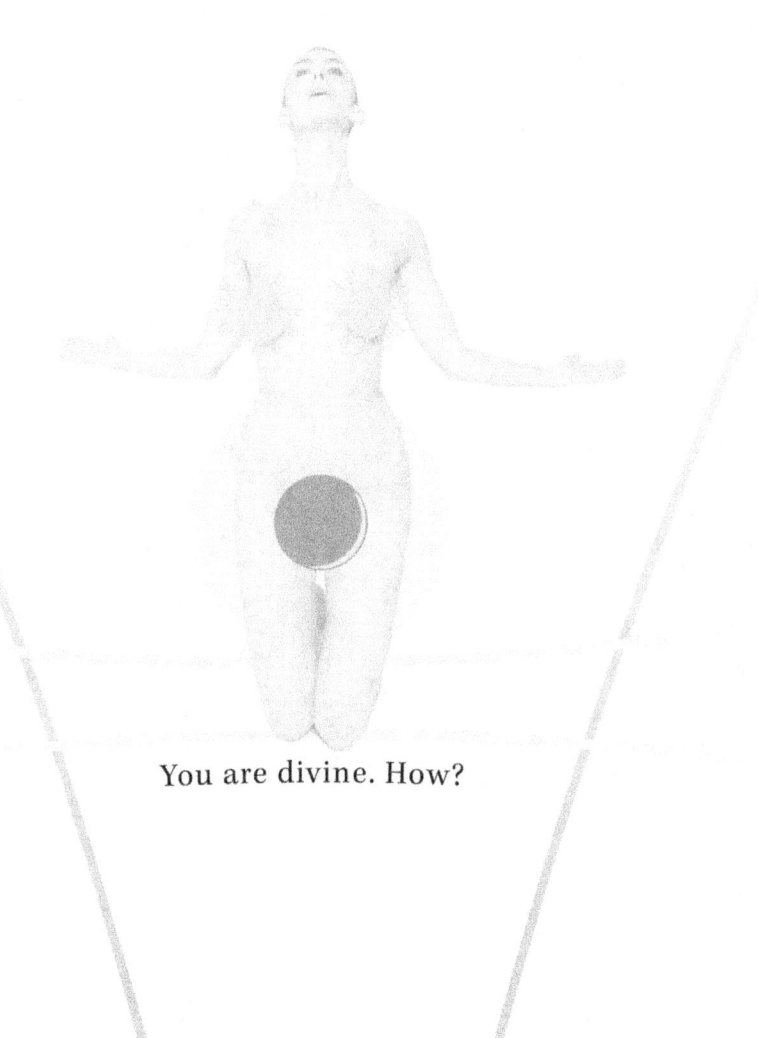

You are divine. How?

What
stories
or
wishes
do the
words
playground
and
recess
inspire?

What if
you're
doing
your
best
right
now?

When does structure support your creative or playful self?

How do you love to play? Who do you love to play with?

What is "fun" to you?

Has your heart ever exploded?

Tell the story of being a love bomb.

How does responsibility smother your fire?

Describe
a costume
you'd like
to wear,
and
where
you'd
like to
wear it.

What have you learned about yourself?

What are you still exploring?

When do you struggle to express yourself?

{flip & continue}

YOU ARE FUCKING AWESOME.

Big love to my witting & unwitting teachers

- Heidi Rose Robbins
- Lauren Fitzgerald
- Julia Cameron
- Elizabeth Gilbert
- Brené Brown
- Esther Perel
- Ibram X. Kendi
- Michael Bean
- Kara Swisher
- Dossie Easton
- Haruki Murakami
- Robin Wall Kimmerer
- Robert A. Heinlein
- Lauren Crow
- M
- Harriet Lerner
- Marshall Rosenberg
- Elle Luna
- Austin Kleon
- Mark Manson
- James P. Carse
- Simon Sinek
- Medhi Hasan
- Janet Hardy
- wecouldgrowup2gether
- The Schneider Family

If this book

inspired

you

please

pass it on   to someone

you

wish

to

inspire.

-Simon Sinek

The infinite Game

About the Creator

Wyoh is a multidisciplinary artist committed to creating a more compassionate, sustainable world in which mutual love and inspiration is the norm, and everyone has access to the resources they need to give their unique gifts.

wyohlee.com

www.ingramcontent.com/pod-product-compliance
Lightning Source LLC
Chambersburg PA
CBHW080037120526
44589CB00037B/2726